GLOBAL
AMERICA

ALSO BY JOHN MANZELLA

Grasping Globalization: Its Impact and Your Corporate Response

Mexico & NAFTA: The Real Impact

Opportunity in Mexico: A Small Business Guide

Breaking Into the Trade Game (updated)

Trade and Finance For Lenders

Export: Map Your International Textile Trade Strategy

The Business Guide to Free Trade: A Comprehensive Analysis of the U.S.-Canada Free Trade Agreement

GLOBAL AMERICA

Understanding Global and
Economic Trends and How To
Ensure Competitiveness

JOHN MANZELLA

For additional copies of this book, visit
www.GlobalAmerica.ManzellaTrade.com

ISBN 978-0-926566-01-9 (soft cover)
ISBN 978-0-926566-05-7 (e-book)

Library of Congress Control Number: 2015910016

Published by
Manzella Trade Communications, Inc.
PO Box 1188, Williamsville, NY 14231-1188
Info@ManzellaTrade.com www.ManzellaTrade.com
Tel: (716) 983-7081

Book and cover design by Jon Guevara

Global America will give you a no-holds-barred view of the near and long-term effects of some of the most recent economic trends today. This book is essential reading for everyone interested in the new complex global factors and drivers of productivity and prosperity.
Barbara Osterman, Founder and Owner of Human Solutions LLC.

John Manzella presents a cogent, comprehensive picture of the emerging demographic and economic trends shaping the future of globalization and offers smart policy recommendations and business strategies for competing successfully in a rapidly changing international environment.
Daniel Ikenson, Director of The Cato Institute's
Herbert A. Stiefel Center for Trade Policy Studies

John Manzella has written a thought provoking book that explores the many perils that exist in the international business landscape, how they remain in a state of constant change, and reminds us how important it is to remain fluent in current affairs in order to stay a step ahead of that change. Any business person actively engaged in international business would benefit from reading this book.
Daniel Wagner, CEO of Country Risk
Solutions and Author of Managing Country Risk

Manzella's Global America is an eminently readable and realistic analysis and appraisal of America in the future global economy. While policy is never far from the main discourse, the cherry on the Sundae is his ability to single out key trends and make them meaningful to each us whether we are involved with marketing goods, managing supply chains, investing our savings, or raising our children.

Larry Davidson, Professor Emeritus of Business Economics and Public Policy at the Indiana University Kelley School of Business

John Manzella's book Global America is just the right antidote for the misguided belief that Americans cannot prosper in a global economy. Based on thorough research and his years of experience in global consulting, Manzella explodes myth after myth about such charged topics as immigration, NAFTA, and trade with China. His prescription of more open markets, property rights, the rule of law, and education and tax reform points to a brighter future.

Daniel Griswold, President of the National Association of Foreign-Trade Zones

In Global America, John does an excellent job of providing a timely snapshot of America's competitive position vis-a-vis the global economy — 15 years into the 21st century. This book provides an island of context in an all too temporal sea of tweets and spin.

Greg Sandler, President of ThinkGlobal Inc.

This book is dedicated to my wife, Karla, who always supports my endeavors, and to my children, Lauren, Christopher, Victoria and Francesca, who I encourage to follow their dreams regardless of how difficult they may seem.

ACKNOWLEDGMENTS

I would like to express my appreciation to all those who made this book possible. I am particularly grateful to the following individuals for their insightful comments, assistance and guidance: Jon Guevara, Ryan Wolf, Ralph Watkins, Chuck Banas, Daniel Ikenson, Larry Davidson, Louis Manzella, Christopher McKee, David Hofmann, Barbara Osterman, Daniel Griswold, Daniel Wagner, Tim Ebsary, John Rowney, Greg Sandler, Bob Rice, Jeff Belt, Peter Mack, Joel Goldberg, George Leone, Ed Wilmot, Doug Bandow, Neal Asbury, Shawn Mahoney, Sam Baker, Vincent LoTempio, Anita Rosen, Evan Ellis, Frank Ryll, Jeff Liebel, Jim Dorn, Jim Wilfong, Rich Roffman, Steve Hanke, Hannah Hayes, Chip Thomas, Sung Lee, John DeLuca, and Charlie Goodwin.

CONTENTS

CHAPTER FOUR   59

U.S. PRODUCTION AND ABUNDANT ENERGY

CHAPTER FIVE   79

GLOBALIZATION IS LIKE FIRE

CHAPTER SIX   113

THE NORTH AMERICAN BLOC

CHAPTER SEVEN   129

THE FUTURE OF A U.S.-CHINA DOMINATED WORLD

CONTENTS

INTRODUCTION

New global and economic trends continue to bombard the United States. Regardless of where they originate — domestically or abroad — business, economic and political forces are spinning across the globe, accelerating and evolving at every turn. And in some cases, trends that began in the United States are adapting to changing environments and returning back home with a deeper impact. In the process these forces are creating new realities that seemingly appear at random.

If you think you're not impacted by global trends — think again! They are effecting virtually every aspect of our lives.

Tip O'Neill, former politician and Speaker of the U.S. House of Representatives from 1977 through 1987, coined the phrase "all politics is local." This belief, which encapsulates the principle that a politician's success is directly tied to his or her ability to satisfy the needs of local constituents, is still repeated in the halls of the U.S. Capitol. But politics may be the only thing that's still local.

Whether you are a senior executive of a company seeking greater U.S. market share or pursuing faster-growing markets abroad, a student trying to obtain the skills that will be required tomorrow, a single mother of two children unknowingly competing with Asian workers, a Wall Street investor trying to predict the stock market's direction, or a Wal-Mart employee struggling to get ahead, you can't escape the impact of what's occurring on the world stage.

For every American company and employee, even those that focus solely on the domestic market, *all business is global.* Why? As the world continues to become more interconnected, a company and its employees can no longer escape the effects of international trends and events. And in many cases, we aren't even aware of world factors in our lives.

For the small farmer in Iowa who may feel isolated from global influences, a deeper look may reveal this: the farm machinery is imported or built with foreign parts improving its quality and price; the genetically modified seeds, fertilizers, chemicals and insecticides are the product of intellectual property partly derived from European and American foreign-born scientists on the cutting edge; the farm hands hired during harvest season are from Central America; or the value of the crops and the currency used to buy them are influenced by a multitude of international factors including world volatility.

Various trends, along with the lackluster recovery from the worst recession since the Great Depression, have revealed critical American flaws. Yet, I continue to witness how the United States still captures the world's imagination.

After dozens of speaking engagements in Mexico in the early 1990s, I found that many in the audience either had an American passport or badly wanted one. When I crossed through *Check Point Charlie* from West Berlin to East Berlin in March 1990, I was told by countless East Germans of their wish to move to the United States to seek a better life. And when visiting China in recent years and speaking with Chinese colleagues in recent months, I sense a heightened patriotism and a new confidence there. Nonetheless, young Chinese I meet often tell me of their desire to study in the United States or permanently move here.

What draws so many to the United States? America's "secret sauce" continues to provide tremendous advantages that no other country can. But changes created by various forces may alter that reality. And politicians may poison the sauce.

Today's global trends — which to a large degree are driven and affected by new technologies and innovations, the worsening skills deficit, "real" unemployment levels, the energy revolution, manufacturing dynamics, backshoring and investment flows, site selection decisions, government dysfunction, demographics shifts, a rapidly changing China, and the direction of global economic growth — are creating daunting challenges and shaping our future. What does this mean to the United States, your business, and our children?

Forces operating on the other side of the planet are increasingly being felt here. And this reality is strengthening — not weakening.

Global America connects the dots so we may better understand what has occurred, and peers into the chain reactions as they unfold so we may more accurately grasp what lies ahead — and prepare for it. Going forward, the ability to make well-informed decisions is paramount. This book also provides key strategies that can be employed to boost competitiveness and influence elected officials. And to a large extent, it focuses on America's younger generation, offering them indispensable guidance because they are the face of the future who must compete with 1.4 billion Chinese, 1.3 billion Indians, and 4.3 billion others around the globe struggling to get ahead.

THE PERILS OF GROWING UP IN A HIGH-TECH WORLD

Although it was decades ago, every May I'm reminded of my own college graduation. In recent years, two of my four children walked across the stage in cap and gown to receive their degrees. But the world they enter is an entirely different place than what I experienced at their age.

THE IMPACT OF NEW TECHNOLOGIES

Today's new innovations and technologies are having a tremendous impact on the United States and the world. The resulting new drivers of growth, which will create trillions of dollars in new economic output, are also disruptive, transforming labor markets, industries, and the global economy at warp speed. Combined with other pressing new economic realities and hyper-global competition, these changes are forcing American companies to redesign business models and delve deeper into their core competencies to create even more innovative products and services for markets across the globe.

As a result, more knowledgeable workers with deeper skill sets increasingly are in demand. A growing number of employees are required to think critically, solve complex analytical problems, and manipulate sophisticated new technologies — a tall order. Yesterday's jobs, like those requiring lower-skilled routine quantitative functions, will continue to move offshore, remain offshore or be automated.

When inexpensive labor is vital, companies have tended to outsource, offshore or relocate their manufacturing activities to the next low-cost country. This trend, which began with the advent of industrialization, observed low-tech production moving from Great Britain to the United States, then to Japan, South Korea, Hong Kong, Taiwan, and in the last few decades, to Mexico, China, and other developing countries. In the process, jobs are lost. But this isn't always the case.

Catherine L. Mann, a professor of economics at Brandeis University and former policy specialist at the Peterson Institute for International Economics, the Federal Reserve Board of Governors, and the President's Council of Economic Advisers at the White House, says the offshoring of computer manufacturing to low cost countries resulted in a 10 to 30 percent drop in computer costs. In turn, sales of PCs soared. This led to a rapid rise in U.S. productivity and added $230 billion in cumulative gross domestic product (GDP) from 1995 through 2002. The result: many new jobs emerged far exceeding those lost to outsourcing.

The need to employ inexpensive labor for competitive reasons or due to labor shortages has a long history. Beginning with World War II, Mexican workers were invited to the United States to harvest crops under the Bracero Program. And, in 1965, Mexico established the Maquiladora program encouraging U.S. companies to assemble goods in Mexico for export to the United States using U.S.-made components and parts. U.S. duties were applied only to the value-added portion in Mexico. The use of lower-cost labor in Mexico helped U.S. companies compete more effectively in North American markets with imports from Asia.

Similarly, with the European Union's Outward Processing program, French, Italian and German companies sent fabric, auto parts and electronic components to Algeria, Tunisia, Spain, and Yugoslavia for assembly and re-export to the European market. Under its Guest Worker Program, Germany allowed the immigration of foreigners to perform low-paying jobs. Japan also took advantage of inexpensive labor in

East Asia, and established production facilities in Korea, Singapore, Thailand, Malaysia, the Philippines, China and, eventually, Vietnam.

Japanese companies used assembly plants in Mexico to reduce the costs of their products shipped to the U.S. market, and assembly plants in Brazil to gain duty-free access to Latin American markets. After the fall of the Berlin Wall, Western European producers gained access to inexpensive labor in Poland, former Czechoslovakia (now the Czech Republic and Slovakia), Hungary and former East Germany.

More recently, a number of factors are driving backshoring — the shifting of U.S. manufacturing activities from China and other developing countries back to the United States. The reasons include higher compensation for workers in coastal provinces of China, the rising value of its currency, the renminbi, also known as the yuan, and increased transportation costs.

Improvements in automation also are having a tremendous effect on labor and decisions concerning where to establish production factories. When production processes are automated, offshoring becomes less attractive as worker hours, as well as the overall cost of a product attributable to labor, are reduced. Today, analysts estimate that the overall labor component of a manufactured product ranges from 6 percent for highly automated products to as high as 30 percent for labor-intensive operations, with an average in the lower to mid-teens. Stated by General Electric CEO Jeffrey Immelt, "If you look at an aircraft engine, the content of labor is probably less than 5 percent. We have two hours of labor in a refrigerator. So it really doesn't matter if you make it in Mexico, the U.S. or China."

Although the percentages for various industries differ, the direction is clear: advances in automation will continue to reduce the overall labor component of a product, and as a result, reduce the number of jobs required to complete a specific task, especially at the lower skilled levels. The upside: because automation empowers fewer workers to produce much more in less time, it boosts efficiency and productivity — important factors in raising standards of living.

But today, it's not just the lower-skilled jobs that are affected. Many higher-skilled knowledge-worker tasks regarded as impossible to automate just a few years ago now are performed by machines with advanced artificial intelligence. And newer computers that have significantly increased computing power while coming down in price can answer unstructured questions posed by customers that were never thought possible a few years ago. To illustrate how far we have come, consider this: the iPhone 4 offers roughly the same performance as a $5 million 1975 supercomputer.[1]

These dynamic changes, which bring opportunity as well as chaos and confusion by upsetting existing methods and ways of doing things, will increasingly affect everyone. And the impact may be more severe than the changes brought forth by industrialization, which emerged in the late 1700s in Great Britain and early 1800s in the United States and Germany. The shift from an agrarian society to an industrial economy created tremendous advantages, as well as anxiety and fear. It compelled workers to leave farms in search of factory jobs and master an entirely new set of skills. The demands placed on young workers today are even steeper and the skills required are much more complex.

It wasn't long ago that nations with an abundance of natural resources had a competitive edge. Today, the only sustainable competitive advantage is knowledge — and with it, the ability of our children to learn faster, apply new technologies better, and boost productivity more quickly than the competition. Moving forward, we all need to adapt since many jobs and industries not on the cutting edge are on the losing end. Consequently, it's no surprise why few companies originally comprising the S&P 500 in 1957 remain on the list. As evolutionary theory goes: it is not the strongest of the species that survives, nor the most intelligent that survives. It is the one that is most adaptable to change.

History is replete with examples of how waves of new innovative technologies significantly boosted efficiencies, enhanced performance and improved our lives. For example, the invention of the steam engine and its application to railroads enabled the speedy transport of mass produced goods, including steel, across large distances. This significantly contributed to the building of the United States. And the harnessing of electricity, which turned night into day, changed virtually every aspect of how we live.

But many innovations, while offering greater value, disrupted markets and industries, and displaced workers. For example, in the early 19th century the English Luddites destroyed textile machines because they replaced weavers. And it's no surprise that automobile workers replaced buggy makers, while ATMs, voice mail and voice recognition software eliminated bank teller, receptionist and medical transcription jobs. It wasn't long ago that many bookstores, camera retailers, film processors, office supply shops, travel agencies, and big box electronics and appliance retailers were replaced by online retailers and the current businesses occupying America's main streets.

THE DEATH OF DISTANCE

American innovation has transformed how work is done. It also has changed how we do business and who we do it with. Technological advances in telecommunications, transportation and finance have led to the integration of national markets through international trade, foreign direct investment and portfolio investment. This process is known as globalization. Since the emergence of local, regional and national economies — initially due to the separation of production and consumption resulting from the cheap transportation of goods via rail — there has been a constant evolution in the stages of cultural and economic development. Globalization, which is another step in that evolution, has empowered companies and individuals to establish relationships anywhere in the world.

With the continual implementation of new sophisticated technologies that eliminate distance, the world is becoming smaller every day as more and more people from all corners of the globe connect. In just a very short period, for example, portable devices like smartphones and tablets have gone from a luxury for a few to a way of life for more than one billion people worldwide. In the United States wireless web use is expected soon to exceed wired use.[2] Using Skype, FaceTime, Viber and other free or inexpensive means to connect the world's best and brightest minds has resulted in greater global cooperation and, in turn, created new value as new products and services are quickly designed and distributed around the world.

Due to this and a number of other reasons, an increasingly greater share of economic growth is occurring outside the United States. And why not? The U.S. population of 321 million only represents 4.4 percent of the world's population of 7.25 billion. To reach the other 95.6 percent, U.S. firms need to expand internationally. In turn, global business and international investment are becoming significantly more important factors in the creation of new economic growth here in the United States and an important generator of jobs. But as U.S. firms promote their products and services abroad, other nations effectively do the same and continue to gain U.S. market share, raising the number of competitors here at home.

When I graduated from college in 1983, I viewed my competition as other Americans. Today, our children's competition includes 7 billion people in all corners of the globe. And since U.S. economic growth rates will remain relatively modest due to a variety of factors, a topic covered later, the "real" unemployment level — which includes those looking for a job, plus those who still desire a job but technically have exited the labor force — will remain elevated for years to come. This means fewer, but more mentally demanding jobs will be available for our brightest graduates.

TECHNOLOGICAL LITERACY AND MILLENNIALS

Today, higher-skilled jobs unlikely to be automated in the foreseeable future — like those that require critical thinking and reasoning, as well as abstract analytical, intuitive and creative problem solving skills — are in greater demand. But herein lies the problem: there are too few people with the right skill sets to satisfy demand in the United States. Unfortunately, this problem is getting worse as today's new technologies — including green industries, cloud storage and faster computing, smart phones and tablets, apps, hydraulic fracturing, 3D printing, advanced materials and robotics, energy storage, nanotechnology, and biotechnology — require more knowledgeable and highly skilled employees to develop, refine and operate.

Long gone are the days when one could obtain a job and perform the same tasks with the same skill set for decades before retiring. The changes new technologies usher in are accelerating, especially when entrepreneurs introduce products and processes that replace existing profitable ones that still have shelf life. The benefits of this are explained by Joseph Schumpeter, the Austrian American economist and political scientist who popularized the term "creative destruction." According to Schumpeter, the new will destroy the old even if the old is still valuable.

Innovation by entrepreneurs is extremely important. It is the force that sustains long-term economic growth and the energy that fuels the private sector, even as the process destroys the value of existing organizations. This economically beneficial process further pressures workers by accelerating skills cycles, which already have fallen from years to mere months. This forces employees of every age and skill level to engage in the practice of life-long learning.

When it comes to this, the United States has a significant advantage. Due to the nature of our universities, their structure, number and the openness with which they operate, the United States continues to lead the world in post-secondary education. And these factors can't easily be duplicated around the world.

But many of America's educational problems lie at the primary and secondary levels. As a result, large numbers of American students and tremendous numbers of dropouts are unprepared for the higher levels of competition ahead. At the high school level, for example, many politicians and parents are quick to blame teachers and administrators for failing schools and graduation rates among the lowest in the industrialized world. But a major part of the problem lies with a culture of indifference, where many students are unmotivated and disruptive, and often create a hostile environment that makes learning difficult.

Compounding this problem are parents who often don't support our high schools' disciplinary efforts, further weakening an already impotent system fearful of racial and socio-economic divides. What's more, many "helicopter parents" — those who hover over their children's every move, making everything OK and covering up for their kids' failures — have become "drone parents" — those who attack teachers that don't reward their children with the grades parents believe are deserved. In many cases, teachers and administrators feel pressure to comply or face distracting law suits and bad press.

When I grew up in the 1960s and 1970s, we didn't receive trophies for showing up; we received trophies for winning. And if teachers called our parents with news of a poor attitude or bad grades, our parents didn't want to hear our side of the story. The teachers were not questioned; we simply were punished. Our parents' generation understood that without a fundamental understanding of what is required to compete and win, we wouldn't learn how to struggle and lose. And as many of us well know, learning how to accept failure is often part of a successful process.

Unfortunately, much of America's youth has been shielded from failure and is unaware of its true value until it's too late. This often is reflected in the collapse of family businesses at the third generation. In many cases, the father had started a business, worked long hours and understood the value of a dollar. The son or daughter, often working alongside, inherited these traits and continued to build the business. Then, years later, after spending little time in the trenches, the often pampered grandson or granddaughter steps in with a sense of entitlement. It's no surprise that this third generation typically doesn't know what it takes to run a business, and in turn, runs it into the ground.

This entitlement mentality, to some degree, is reflected in the millennial generation, also referred to as generation Y, defined as those born after 1980 through about 2000. When 1,000 adults were asked in a 2014 Reason-Rupe survey if the term "entitled" described young people age 18 to 29 years old, 65 percent said it describes this group well. Much of the fault lies with us, the "helicopter" parents, who grew up in a post-60s era when the pendulum began to swing from a conservative era to a liberal one.

On the other hand, Millennials appear to be more socially conscious than their predecessors, and very concerned about social and economic sustainability. In fact, surveys indicate that when buying products or considering employers to work for, this generation values the degree to which companies are socially responsible. Millennials make up nearly 40 percent of the current workforce and are at a pace to reach 75 percent by 2025.[3]

Millennials are different from other generations in other ways as well. According to a study by PriceWaterhouseCoopers, a global consulting firm, "Millennials have a greater expectation to be supported and appreciated in return for their contributions, and to be part of a cohesive team. Flexibility in where they work and how much they work is also a key driver in Millennial satisfaction. This view differs in importance from that of the non-Millennial generation, which places greater importance on pay and development opportunities."

Pew Research describes Millennials as "relatively unattached to organized politics and religion, linked by social media, burdened by debt, distrustful of people, in no rush to marry and optimistic about the future." Millennials tend to vote Democratic and hold liberal views on many political and social issues, are very comfortable with technology, and have become accustomed to receiving information instantaneously, says Pew Research.

Nielsen, a leading global provider of information and insights, says "Millennials like having the world at their fingertips. With the resurgence of cities as centers of economic energy and vitality, a majority are opting to live in urban areas over the suburbs or rural communities. Sixty-two percent indicate they prefer to live in the type of mixed-use communities found in urban centers, where they can be close to shops, restaurants and offices." As a result, Nielsen says, "For the first time since the 1920s growth in U.S. cities outpaces growth outside of them." This trend certainly is good for cities, which for years experienced a decline in population as an increasing number of families moved to the suburbs.

On the economic side of the equation, Pew Research says Millennials are "the first in the modern era to have higher levels of student loan debt, poverty and unemployment, and lower levels of wealth and personal income than their two immediate predecessor generations (generation x and baby boomers) had at the same stage of their life cycles." Much of this is attributable to the Great Recession.

According to Pew Research, one-third of Millennials, ages 26 to 33, have a four-year degree or better and, as a result, are the best educated young adults in American history. At the same time, there is a mismatch between much of the knowledge attained in school and knowledge required in the workplace.

THE WORSENING KNOWLEDGE CRISIS

As a result of the knowledge mismatch and a multitude of other factors, the United States has experienced a skills shortage that is getting increasingly worse. For example, in 2012, although the U.S. unemployment rate was approximately 8 percent, 600,000 U.S. manufacturing jobs still went unfilled.[4]

In late 2013, the Dallas Federal Reserve identified an "acute labor shortage" in a variety of job categories. And a 2014 report published by Accenture, a global management consulting firm, and the Manufacturing Institute, the research arm of the National Association of Manufacturers, indicated that more than 75 percent of manufacturers surveyed indicated a moderate to severe shortage of "skilled" labor, while more than 80 percent of respondents reported a moderate to severe shortage of "highly skilled" labor. Plus, a 2014 Vistage survey said nearly one third of all CEOs surveyed indicated staffing needs as the most critical of issues facing their business.

In a 2014 article, Stephen Moore, an economist and former member of *The Wall Street Journal* editorial board, said overall, there are at least one million jobs that can't be filled in the United States due to a lack of skills. And these jobs are not necessarily the most sophisticated either. Moore identified various positions, including driving jobs that pay $50,000 and up, and estimated there were 30,000 to 50,000 too few truckers to run long haul routes. What's more, the American Trucking Association reportedly indicated that the shortage could top 200,000 drivers in the next decade. In sum, the shortage in a variety of industries at all skill levels will get worse as the economy improves and the need for workers grows.

More recent surveys reflect similar conditions. For example, a 2015 Deloitte Manufacturing Institute study says six out of ten manufacturing positions currently remain vacant and projects that 2 million manufacturing jobs will remain unfilled over the next decade, a significant number considering the total number of jobs demanded will be nearly 3.5 million. According to Deloitte, such a shortage is significant and can have a material impact on manufacturers' growth and profitability. Thus, 82 percent of executives surveyed said they believe the skills gap will impact their ability to meet customer demand, and 78 percent indicated it will impact their ability to implement new technologies and increase productivity. Executives surveyed also said the skills gap impacts their "ability to provide effective customer service (69 percent), the ability to innovate and develop new products (62 percent), and the ability to expand internationally (48 percent)."

Companies are not the only group feeling the effects of too few workers with the right stuff. Miriam Jordan, a senior special writer in the Los Angeles bureau of *The Wall Street Journal,* said more than two-thirds of America's youth would fail to qualify for military service due to physical, behavioral or educational shortcomings. She cited obesity, lack of a high school diploma, felony convictions, and drug use as some of the reasons.

Other factors contributing to the worsening skills deficit include the fact that baby boomers, those born between 1946 and 1964, continue to retire in droves. The problem: they are taking their skills with them. In addition, after reaching their highest labor force participation rate of 60 percent in 1999, participation among women has declined.[5]

Plus, due to an inability of many people to sell their homes at pre-recession assessed values, fewer are able to relocate to seek or accept new jobs. Furthermore, much of America's youth are staying put. Thus, in 2014 the U.S. Census Bureau said the mobility of adults aged 25 to 29 was at a 50-year low, largely a result of the Great Recession and the ongoing period of slow economic growth. Reduced mobility by the young is illustrated by the fact that, after accounting for new arrivals, from 2004 through 2007 an average of 50,000 people aged 25 to 34 left both New York City and Los Angeles annually. However, from 2010 through 2013, fewer than 23,000 of this cohort left New York City and approximately 12,000 left Los Angeles.[6]

Moving forward, two levels of young workers are becoming apparent: the highly qualified and the totally unqualified. And the costs are staggering. If the United States had closed the international achievement gap between 1983 and 1998 and raised the performance of its primary and secondary education to the level of Finland and Korea, U.S. GDP in 2008 would have been between $1.3 trillion and $2.3 trillion higher.[7] The ripple effect from closing the achievement gap today would be much greater. The bottom line: if workers with the necessary skills and/or attitude can't be found, corporate growth potential will be limited. To solve this problem, many firms will be forced to move to new domestic or foreign locations where the right combination of skills exists.

JOBS, EDUCATION AND THE RIGHT STUFF

Today's unemployment trends are favorable. Nevertheless, many looking for a job say the task doesn't seem any easier. Why? Government statistics don't always reflect what is actually occurring on the ground. For example, in May 2014 the number of Americans working climbed back to its high of 146 million in 2007, just before the Great Recession began, and in June 2015 reached 148.7 million, the U.S. Department of Labor reported. This "good news" was tempered, however, by two trends.

WHAT WE CAN LEARN FROM CURRENT UNEMPLOYMENT DATA

Many of the jobs gained have been lower-paying, part-time positions that replaced higher-paying, full-time positions. And if one higher-paying 40 hour a week full-time job with benefits was eliminated and replaced by two 20 hour a week part-time jobs at lower pay and without benefits, the net gain was one job and the statistics appeared improved. But did the situation really get better as statistics might indicate? In the process, important skills were lost. This trend continues today.

In addition to this trend, a second trend is even more telling. From the beginning of 2007 through the end of 2014, another 19 million people entered the civilian non-institutional population. This group, which includes people 16 years of age or older who are not in the armed forces, incarcerated or in homes for the elderly, continues to expand each year. Unfortunately, during this period, the number of newly created jobs simply did not keep pace with those entering the labor force. From this fact alone, one would have expected the unemployment rate to increase and not decrease as it did. Why? The tremendous number of frustrated job seekers who stopped looking for work were no longer counted in the work force, and therefore, no longer considered in the official unemployment rate.

Today, there still are millions of people who technically are not in the work force but want a job. When added to those who technically are unemployed and by definition, currently seeking a job, the total number of people out of work — a figure the Department of Labor indicates in its lessor knows U-4 and U-5 categories, and what I refer to as "real" unemployment — is considerably higher than the official unemployment rate. And when delving deeper, other factors become apparent.

For example, in June 2015, the participation rate, the percent of the civilian non-institutional population considered in the work force, was 62.6 percent, the lowest since the late 1970s. Dragging this down, of course, were the large numbers of frustrated workers who could not find a job and technically have exited the labor force. Another significant factor was the vast number of baby boomers born between 1946 and 1964 who continue to retire in droves.

Of all the age groups, young Americans continue to experience perhaps the most difficulty. And many adults agree that this could last for quite some time. A 2014 *Wall Street Journal*/NBC poll said 76 percent of adults lack the confidence that their children's generation will have a better life than they do — an all-time high.

What will the situation be in the coming years? Surprising to many, the participation rates for all of America's young age groups — those aged 16 to 19, 20 to 24 and 25 to 34 — are projected to decline through 2022, the latest year reviewed by a Bureau of Labor Statistics study. And the participation rates of the next older age groups, 35 to 44 and 45 to 54, also are projected to decline through 2022. In a reversal of past decades, each age group 55 and older is projected to experience the opposite — an increase in participation rates through 2022, the Bureau of Labor Statistics says. Why?

These relatively new trends may be the result of the desire or need of older Americans to remain in the labor force for longer periods of time, especially if full retirement is not financially feasible. In turn, this leaves fewer jobs available for younger workers, pushing their participation rates lower. Another contributing factor lowering participation rates among America's young is an increase in school attendance. But this has a big upside.

Overall, in June 2015, the participation and unemployment rates of those 25 years and older were 44.6 and 8.2 percent, respectively, for those without a high school diploma, 57.1 and 5.4 percent for those with a high school diploma, 66.8 and 4.2 percent for those with some college or an associate degree, and 74.6 and 2.5 percent for those with a bachelor's degree or higher. It stands to reason: the least skilled are the least likely to find a job in this knowledge-based economy and therefore more likely to exit the labor force.

Without an understanding of the participation rate, the unemployment rate is not very meaningful. And if job seekers continue to become frustrated, they too will exit the labor force making the employment picture appear better than it actually is. On the other hand, there are those that meet the participation requirements but have no intention of actually working.

A number of physically non-needy people have determined that a job they are likely to find will pay less than what they can accumulate in government handouts, such as food stamps, housing subsidies, mortgage assistance, health insurance subsidies, etc. In turn, some recruiters have indicated that applicants apply for positions without any intention of accepting them simply to satisfy "looking for a job" unemployment requirements. The result: the government inadvertently has created incentives to keep people at home rather than at work.

Many wonder what it will take to get the "real" unemployment rate back to 5 to 6 percent, a level considered normal prior to the recent recession which began in 2008. To do so, as well as accommodate new entrants into the labor force, the United States would need to create 21 million net new jobs within this decade.[1] This figure breaks down to the creation of 175,000 jobs each month for 10 years. The Bureau of Labor Statistics reports that nonfarm payroll employment increased an average of 194,000 per month in 2013 and 246,000 per month in 2014 — good numbers. Unfortunately, the economy has never gained 21 million new jobs in any decade.

Thus, 20.9 million net jobs were created in the 1970s, 18.5 million in the 1980s, 16.1 million in the 1990s, and 5.6 million in the last decade, according to the Labor Department's Household data. Of course, many factors impact these numbers, including the growth rate of the civilian non-institutional population, trends in the number of retirees, and the number of immigrants and women entering and departing the workforce. Nonetheless, given historical precedent, the creation of so many jobs on a long-term basis is a formidable challenge.

PREPARING OUR YOUTH FOR THE GLOBAL BATTLE AHEAD

The United States led the world in expanding access to high school, and following World War II, in access to college. By 1950, 53 percent of the population aged 25 to 29 had completed high school or higher; by 2013 this had risen to 90 percent. For college and higher, it rose from 8 percent in 1950 to 34 percent in 2013.[2] In turn, through greater access to education, the American labor force became the world's most productive and innovative.

These gains had a tremendous positive impact. Stated by Jacob Kirkegaard, author of *The Accelerating Decline in America's High Skilled Workforce*, "America rose to economic prominence on the shoulders of the most highly skilled workforce in the world." However, during the last few decades, skill levels in the U.S. workforce have stagnated and, as previously stated, now are causing a skills deficit at many levels. The reasons for this are many.

Due to American demographic shifts, there are fewer high school graduates. A growing segment are asking whether or not college is worth the cost — and for good reason. From 1984 to 2015, inflation-adjusted tuition and fees at four-year public and private non-profit institutions has risen 225 and 146 percent, respectively.[3] As a result, college has become out of reach for many. And for those who do attend four-year American universities, many are saddled with tremendous debt.

This is compounded by the fact that students typically complete more than a dozen credit hours than is necessary to obtain a bachelor's degree. But much more surprisingly, only 36 percent graduate in four years and less than 60 percent in six years.[4] In addition, today there are an increasing number of non-traditional students that include older, as well as more ethnically diverse students, with broader socioeconomic backgrounds. And in many cases, non-traditional students are unprepared for college-level study and incur higher dropout rates.

To boost the number of college and university graduates with the necessary skill sets to satisfy growing demand by U.S.-based corporations, foreign students studying at U.S. colleges and universities could help fill that gap if they were allowed to remain in the United States after graduation or after achieving a master's degree. How important is this? Consider the fact that more than half of the corporate start-ups in Silicon Valley between 1995 and 2005 were founded by immigrants.[5] Today, there is no question that immigrants play a very significant role in the development of American innovation and corporate success.

There is virtually an endless supply of foreigners who wish to attend American universities. And the number of those currently studying in the United States is large. As of February 2015, there were 1.13 million foreign students attending American universities. Approximately three-quarters of these students were enrolled in bachelor's, master's or doctoral programs. Since the terrorist attacks of September 11, 2001, when the United States restricted student visas, the numbers have significantly increased.[6]

Currently, Asia is the largest source of students, at 855,807, followed by Europe, at 91,567, North America (Canada and Mexico), at 74,602, South America, at 54,724, and Africa, at 49,552. Broken down, China is the source of 331,371 students, followed by India, with

146,336 students, South Korea, 87,384, and Saudi Arabia, 80,941.[7]

U.S. colleges and universities, which are the world's best, attract the brightest students from all corners of the globe. According to the 2014 Academic Ranking of World Universities at the Center for World-Class Universities of Shanghai Jiao Tong University, 36 American universities rank in the world's top 55. This is not bad considering the United States represents only 4.4 percent of the world's population. However, a U.S. immigration policy that educates the world's best and brightest and then sends them home to compete against us is, in my opinion, a failed policy.

FINDING AND RETAINING THE BEST EMPLOYEES

To a large degree, the future success of American businesses depends on their ability to find and retain talented employees who can learn new skills quickly and implement increasingly sophisticated technologies. And due to the corporate trend of focusing on core competencies, the depth and range of skills required of employees will only increase.

In addition, since more and more U.S. companies need to expand globally to remain competitive, employees need to be well versed in the ways of the world, not just in ways of the United States. Consequently, it is imperative to have an understanding of foreign business, economics, and politics, as well as foreign cultures and languages. And the more knowledge an employee has in this arena, the more valuable and likely he or she will be to write his or her own ticket.

What functions may be required? A purchasing manager in a U.S. manufacturing multinational, for example, may be required to source inputs from around the world to support its production facilities in Asia and North America. To do this, the employee would need advanced skills in a host of information technologies, the ability to coordinate the activities of colleagues and business partners in a global network, and very likely formal education in foreign languages.

To find and retain the best candidates, employers will need to create more attractive working conditions and compensation programs, offer incentives with tangible short-term benefits, invest more in employee training efforts, and continually refresh and upgrade employee skills. In addition, to ensure courses offered satisfy market demands and to eliminate what many employers consider a work-skills mismatch, companies need to work more closely with local universities, community colleges and trade schools.

Company partnerships with trade schools

and community colleges, as well as graduate schools, has been occurring for some time. However, what is newer and necessary is the teaming up of companies and traditional undergraduate schools. Examples of this include Northrop Grumman and the University of Maryland, who have teamed up to educate students on cybersecurity, and the partnering of International Business Machines Corp. and Ohio State to train students in data analytics.

Moving forward, American academic institutions at all levels must design new educational strategies that emphasize critical thinking over rote memorization. And since skills need to be continually upgraded, inexpensive and far reaching online learning programs sponsored by universities, community colleges and companies can be expanded to help re-educate workers. The academic community agrees.

In a survey of 2,800 colleges and universities in 2013 by The Babson Survey Research Group, 66 percent of chief academic leaders said online learning is critical to their long term strategies. This figure, which has risen from 49 percent in 2002 when the survey was first conducted, and piqued in 2012 at 69 percent, indicates a clear shift in educational thinking. And many of the institutions are following through. The same survey indicates that 60 percent of post-secondary institutions now offer online courses as demand for this is increasing more quickly than demand for traditional classes. Online learning also offers colleges and universities new sources of revenue as the number of traditional students decline.

Founded in 1976 by John Sperling, PhD, a Cambridge-educated economist and professor-turned-entrepreneur, the University of Phoenix has more than 100 locations across the United States and world, and offers a tremendous number of online classes. In an interview with the *Phoenix Business Journal* on October 21, 2014, Greg Cappelli, CEO of Apollo Education Group, which owns the University of Phoenix, said "We have 25 million to 30 million people who are underemployed, sitting on the sidelines." He continued, "I talk to Fortune 500 CEOs coast to coast who say they can't get the right people to fill the jobs quickly and efficiently."

As a result, the University of Phoenix has relationships with 3,000 companies and most Fortune 500 firms in an attempt to help them reduce the skills gap and educate their employees in a manner that is convenient to the student. I was quoted in the same article noting the importance of companies like Apollo in the effort to reduce the skills deficit.

The push by parents and educators for all students to attend college, and an American cultural attitude that looks down on those that don't attend college is a blunder.

For many youths with varying abilities and aptitudes, the emphasis may be better focused on the skilled trades and careers such as machinist, welder, electrician, carpenter and plumber. What's more, there is a shortage of people in these fields. This is obvious to many homeowners who try to find the labor they need, and when they do, pay a premium.

When it comes to the trades, we certainly can learn from the Europeans, where 70 percent of the youth age 15 through 19 in Switzerland, 65 percent in Germany, and 55 percent in Austria are involved in apprenticeships covering hundreds of occupations.[8] Germany, which is widely recognized for excellent vocational training, has done a relatively good job matching employee skills with corporate needs. From a cultural standpoint, working as an apprentice and ultimately accepting a career in the trades is widely perceived as a worthy pursuit.

But for those students where college is the best choice, data still indicate that it is well worth the tuition. In 2012, the median annual income of full-time workers age 25 to 34 with a Bachelor's degree or higher was nearly $50,000; for those receiving a high school diploma, nearly $30,000.[9] Over a lifetime, workers with a Bachelor's degree earned on average well over $1 million more than those with a high school diploma.[10]

Whether a trade certificate, associate, bachelor's

or advanced university degree is sought, there still is no substitute to simply putting in the hours — and a lot of them. According to Malcolm Gladwell, author of *Outliers*, the number of hours of practice necessary to become an expert in a field is roughly 10,000. Throughout his book, Gladwell repeatedly refers to his 10,000-hour rule, which he claims is the necessary amount of time to really master a specific task.

Many retirees have achieved well over 10,000 hours of practice and subsequent expertise in their fields. But as noted earlier, when they retire they take their skills with them. Employers are wise not to overlook those who have retired but still are interested in working full time, part time or on a consulting basis. And since older Americans are living longer, healthier lives, many are willing and able to contribute well after their first retirement.

When the right skills simply can't be found, human resource executives often tell me they are willing to hire a candidate if he or she possesses a good attitude and willingness to learn. This always reminds me of my high school days, where much of the academic success I witnessed was not by the naturally gifted students, but by those who possessed a positive attitude, real drive, and a determination to do what was necessary to overcome the obstacles they faced. And I certainly can relate to this.

Being diagnosed with dyslexia at a young age, I was told by my father that I would have to work twice as hard as the other students to receive good grades. I had no choice but to accept this, and did well, but not great in school. In fact, having found strategies to cope, years passed during grammar school, high school and college when I actually forgot I had dyslexia. In fact, I was only reminded of my limitation when I took standardized tests, which typically resulted in scores well below average. Although very frustrating at times, this didn't dissuade me.

My favorite quote is by Henry Ford, who said "Whether you think you can, or you think you can't, you're right." Believing in yourself often is three-quarters of the struggle. And it's easier to believe in yourself when one puts in the hours and gains the confidence of that experience. Unfortunately, too many students are quick to discount their abilities and give up — not allowing themselves to fail and learn from that failure.

THE DIRECTION OF ECONOMIC GROWTH

A number of domestic and global trends continue to put downward pressure on the American economy. At the same time, other trends and forces are giving economic growth a boost. This interplay, which often is reflected in the stock market's level of volatility, has left many confused and unsure what's next. However, an analysis of these driving factors and trends reveals much about where we are headed.

NEW INNOVATIVE DRIVERS

Intellectual property, referred to by some as creations of the mind that can be incorporated into tangible objects, has become the primary source of competitive advantage for both companies and countries. Intellectual property can be employed to drive innovation, and in turn, boost productivity, contributing to increased corporate profits, job creation, national economic growth, wages, and standards of living.

Intellectual property, innovation and productivity — defined as the value of output produced by a unit of labor or capital — are key to growth. In recent years, however, the growth rate in non-farm productivity decreased from 2.6 percent during 2000 to 2007 to 1.4 percent during 2007 to 2014, the Bureau of Economic Analysis says. There are many possible reasons why.

Since the recent recession began, companies have tended to hunker down and invest less in new technologies and processes. Plus, many recently developed technologies have focused on consumer products that don't necessarily improve work-related efficiencies. But there may be more impactful trends operating here.

The development and implementation of past innovations, like the cotton gin, steam engine, railroads, telephone, electricity, petrochemicals, internal combustion engine, and plastics all led to increases in efficiency and, in turn, productivity. But many economists say the gains from these innovations — as well as the more recent ones, including pharmaceuticals, computers and the internet — have piqued and will continue to decline, contributing less to productivity growth. I disagree, but admit we may be in a lull.

Productivity gains captured from dated innovations likely are declining. But I would argue that new and innovative applications derived from computers and the internet still are in their infancy and, at this stage, difficult to measure. And the next big innovations on the scene, like green industries, cloud storage and greater computing power, smart phones and tablets, hydraulic fracturing, 3D printing, advanced materials and robotics, energy storage, nanotechnology and biotechnology also are in their early stages of growth. Although their effect on the economy has been relatively minimal to date, their impact over the long term could be a significant driving force for economic growth.

Consumer Confidence and Spending

Many economists referred to the period following the Great Recession as the "new normal." This is distinguished by lower consumption as a share of GDP, lower U.S. household debt, and lower economic growth, as well as higher levels of unemployment and personal savings rates. Although the "new normal" has numerous sustainable benefits, companies, employees and communities have and will continue to undergo difficult transitions to accommodate the impact.

Due to conditions reflected in the "new normal,"

many American consumers still remain concerned about job stability and the strength of the overall economy, and as a result, are not as confident about their future as they were prior to the recession. And there's good reason. Although the recovery is underway, few say they feel the benefits.

In 2013, after adjusting for inflation, the median household income was $51,939. This means half the population made more and half made less than this. The problem: this figure is considerably less than it was in 2007, before the recession began, and about the same as was registered in 1995, according to data from the U.S. Bureau of Census.

The public's uncertainty about the country's economic future continues to be echoed in surveys. For example, in a January 2015 survey by *The Wall Street Journal* and NBC News, only about four in 10 said they were satisfied with the state of the economy. And reported in a March 2015 Pew Research Center survey, 63 percent said the U.S. economic situation is no more secure than it was before the 2008 financial crisis, and a majority said they still believed the economy is vulnerable to another crisis. The bottom line: although the economic situation is improving and attitudes are changing, many Americans continue to be frustrated with their personal financial situation, describe themselves as "treading water," and view the economy as poor.

Consequently, many Americans continue to spend less, save more and pay off debts. This activity is beneficial to household balance sheets. But since consumer spending, known as personal consumption expenditures, represents approximately 70 percent of GDP, any decrease will continue to negatively impact overall economic growth.

Another important factor impacting confidence involves home ownership. The massive decline in housing values throughout the recession, which translated into a deterioration in the largest assets of many, reduced the wealth of millions of Americans. Although home prices nationwide have improved significantly, at the end of the first quarter 2015, 5.1 million homeowners still owed more on their homes than their homes were worth. This represented 10.2 percent of all residential properties with mortgages. Plus another 1.3 million borrowers had less than 5 percent equity.[1]

As the housing market continues to improve, many are unaware of just how far we need to go to climb out of the hole. For example, in 2014, the total value of residential new-builds were slightly more than half of what they were in 2005, the highest year of new builds to date. Stated by Neil Irwin, senior economics correspondent for *The New York Times*, "Even years after the housing burst, the United States is building far fewer houses than would be expected given demographic trends."

One reason: many young adults have delayed home purchases. Paying down college loans, poor job prospects or jobs that just aren't paying enough are factors that have contributed to a reluctance or inability to take on a home mortgage. Consequently, many still live with their parents. This is reflected in a 2014 Pew Research report that indicated roughly one-in-four young adults age 25 to 34 lived in multi-generational households, up from 18.7 percent in 2007 and 11 percent in 1980.

Secondly, as U.S. industry struggles to regain and maintain momentum, many companies continue to remain unsure of future economic growth, and their corporate liabilities in terms of taxes and employee health care premiums. As a result, many continue to hold cash, invest more cautiously and resist hiring.

In some cases, CEOs indicated they were trying to keep their number of employees under the threshold mandated by the Affordable Care Act, known as Obamacare, so as not to be subject to the employer mandate and have to pay for employee health care. Thus, it's not surprising that 25.9 percent of Texas manufacturers surveyed by the Dallas Federal Reserve in

2014 said they were employing fewer workers due to the Affordable Care Act. This practice continue today.

GOVERNMENT DYSFUNCTION

U.S. economic growth has and continues to suffer for other reasons as well. For example, the inability of Congress and President Obama to initially deal with the debt ceiling, government shutdown, fiscal cliff and sequester raised serious questions about the government's overall level of competence that continue today. The government's failure to invest in infrastructure, restructure entitlement programs, seriously tackle immigration issues or initiate a debate on how to improve education has resulted in little confidence that the government will do the right thing. This has contributed to an environment of uncertainty for companies in terms of future corporate liabilities or the direction of fiscal and monetary policy.

Uncertainty, especially in terms of fiscal policy, can have serious consequences. Since tax policy is partly designed to encourage certain behaviors, its absence encourages others. And the impact of uncertainty may be deeper than many have suspected. For example, many CEOs have indicated that uncertainty has paralyzed their decision-making processes and resulted in their companies failing to invest their profits or hire new employees.

Another factor inhibiting corporate investment in the United States is an antiquated tax code that punishes U.S. firms with excessive rates. Thus, the U.S. federal corporate tax rate, at 35 percent, when added to the average estimated state rate of 4.1 percent, brings the combined tax rate to 39.1 percent — the highest among developed countries. If based in New York, for example, the state rate of 6 percent would bring the total to 41 percent. If not swallowed by the government, this money could otherwise be invested. Plus, the government has created an incentive for U.S. companies to establish headquarters abroad in lower taxed countries.

What's worse: the United States is one of the only countries in the Organisation for Economic Co-operation and Development (OECD) that has a worldwide tax system and not a territorial tax system. This means profits earned abroad are subject to the corporate federal tax when repatriated to the United States. Although a tax credit is typically applied that allows for the amount of tax paid to the foreign government to be subtracted from the amount owed to the United States, this tax system provides yet another incentive to establish corporate headquarters abroad.

As a result, it's easy to understand why U.S. firms

do not wish to repatriate an estimated $2.1 trillion in U.S. corporate profits earned abroad — money that could be invested in American research and development, and in plants and equipment, and used to hire and train new employees. It's also easy to understand why a U.S. firm would be interested in being acquired by an Irish firm, which is subject to a significantly lower 12.5 percent corporate tax rate, and not subject at all to income generated in other parts of the world. Known as a corporate inversion, this type of activity isn't theoretical; it's the basis for many cross-border deals.

How bad is American corporate tax policy? The Tax Foundation, an independent tax policy research organization based in Washington, D.C., says the United States has the 32nd most competitive tax system out of the 34 OECD member countries. According to the Tax Foundation, the U.S. top marginal corporate income tax rate at 39.1 percent is followed by Japan (37 percent), France (34.4 percent), and Portugal (31.5 percent). The lowest top marginal corporate income tax rate in the OECD is found in Ireland (12.5 percent). There are four other countries with rates below 20 percent: the Czech Republic (19 percent), Hungary (19 percent), Poland (19 percent), and Slovenia (17 percent). The OECD average is 25.4 percent, the Tax Foundation says.

In addition to an American corporate tax system

that essentially gives our competitors the edge, a great deal of government revenue collected is used to pay the interest on the national debt. And until spending habits change, servicing the debt will become more difficult as interest rates rise. This, of course, leaves fewer dollars to pay for what's really needed.

Congressional gridlock and an inability of our policymakers to come together to execute necessary reforms to reduce the debt and corporate tax rates, or pass legislation to enhance U.S. competitiveness, is at the root of many current problems. And gerrymandering, the redrawing of congressional districts every decade to assure dominance by one party over the other, is partly responsible.

Prior to the 2014 midterm congressional elections in which the Republican Party boosted its majority in the House of Representatives by picking up 14 additional seats and won the Senate, analysts estimated that a majority of congressional districts were "safe seats" for the incumbent. By definition, this empowers politicians to stake out extreme positions and not seek approval of the moderate-voting public. This argument carried much weight prior to the 2014 midterm elections and still continues to do so today, but perhaps less strongly. The midterm elections, it appears, demonstrated that an extensive period of poor economic growth and limited job gains is more important than party or candidate loyalty, and resulted in highly partisan congressional districts voting for the opposition candidate.

Regardless of the dynamics behind congressional gridlock, this dysfunctional political system — where a Democratic president and Republican Congress maintain sharply competing visions — may be divided to a deeper extent than the period during the Vietnam War. This has made compromise extremely difficult. If our government leaders continue in this manner, and are unable to implement legislation to enhance American competitiveness, economic growth will continue to suffer.

In addition, declining U.S. federal and state government spending, which is beneficial in the long term, will continue to negatively impact overall economic demand in the short term. As noted earlier, a worsening skills deficit exists at various levels. If companies can't find workers with the necessary skills and attitude, corporate growth potential will be limited, and in turn, economic growth will be suppressed.

EUROPEAN AND EMERGING MARKETS

Slower foreign growth and resulting weaker demand for American exports also dampens U.S. economic growth.

Due to various recent trends, many international organizations downgraded economic growth projections for countries across the globe. For example, measured in GDP, China's growth rate, which reached double digits for decades, was projected in July 2015 by the International Monetary Fund to decrease from 7.4 percent in 2014 to 6.8 percent in 2015 and 6.3 percent in 2016. And although emerging market growth rates as a whole are projected to slightly dip from 4.6 percent in 2014 to 4.2 percent in 2015, then rise to 4.7 percent in 2016, they are considerably lower than in the past years.

Surprising to many, reported by the International Monetary Fund, economic growth in advanced economies is anticipated to increase from 1.8 percent in 2014 to 2.1 percent in 2015 and 2.4 percent in 2016. As a result, world growth is estimated to slightly dip from 3.4 percent in 2014 to 3.3 percent in 2015 and rise to 3.8 percent in 2016 — levels still lower than were projected in the past. The bottom line: slower growing markets abroad will continue to curtail American exports and investment, which negatively impacts economic growth at home.

For example, since the 2008 recession began, it has become clear that disruptions in Europe affect U.S.-European trade and investment. Why? Europe is the source of approximately 70 percent of U.S. inbound foreign direct investment on a cumulative basis and the destination of 20 percent of American exports. Due to this tremendous mutual attachment, problems in one continent are felt in the other. And many analysts believe that the situation in Europe, especially in Greece, Italy and France, may get worse in 2015 before it gets better.

Each one of the 28 European Union member countries has a different economy, fiscal discipline, democracy, history, values, and language. The European Union leadership's past attempts to drive one-size-fits-all policies in vastly dissimilar countries — like Greece and Germany — has been no easy task. And, as proven by the recent crisis in the eurozone, for European Union countries that use the euro as their official currency, trying to maintain homogeneous economic disciplines during harsh economic times is even more arduous. This problem certainly is reflected in the difficulties of eurozone members to implement and adhere to eurozone policies. In fact, the resulting volatility in the euro has analysts asking whether the euro is a currency or an experiment.

An underlying problem with many European countries has been their inability to adapt to globalization. When a country recognizes the rules of the free market and globalization, and decides to abide by them, it puts on what author and *New York Times* columnist Thomas Friedman called the "Golden Straitjacket." But to fit,

Friedman said, countries must adhere to various policies to enhance national competitiveness.

The United States began squeezing into the Golden Straitjacket in the 1980s. However, one could argue that Greece, and perhaps Spain, France and Italy, haven't donned the straitjacket or, in some ways, adapted as well to globalization as the United States and northern European countries like Germany, Austria and the Netherlands. As a result, unemployment rates in southern Europe are significantly higher than in the north.

Another factor impacting the European Union's overall health is the fact that Germany's economy is dependent on exports, which represent approximately 50 percent of its GDP. Consequently, Germany overwhelms the European Union's free trade zone with its products, and in turn, stifles the development of other member country industries. To help balance this relationship, Germany would have to boost consumer spending.

As noted, economic growth is projected to rise at a slower pace than in past decades for many developing and emerging economies, including China. There are many reasons for this. For starters, the tremendous credit and commodity booms ended some time ago. Since the Great Recession began, credit has been curbed in the United States and abroad. Plus, as interest rates rise, an inevitability moving forward, credit availability will be impacted to a greater degree. And the demand for commodities, especially by industries in China, has decreased as the Middle Kingdom's economic growth continues to level off. This is unlikely to change in the near future.

Additionally, high levels of volatility and financial problems continue to plague emerging markets and developing countries. Governance problems have re-surfaced. And many of these countries are less open to the implementation of economic reforms that have proven beneficial in the past.[2] Other primary reasons include a decrease in emerging market and developing country exports to advanced economies. This also is unlikely to significantly change in the years ahead.

Furthermore, many emerging markets and developing countries didn't always reciprocate with advanced economies in terms of trade. As a result, moving forward, many advanced economies are negotiating free trade agreements without developing country participation. An example is the Transatlantic Trade and Investment Partnership currently being negotiated with the European Union.

If successful as currently envisioned, the OECD says this deal would cover approximately 50 percent of global output, nearly 30 percent of world merchandise trade, and 20 percent of global foreign investment. Protectionist and nationalistic tendencies in leading emerging economies, such as Brazil and India, will leave these countries on the outside looking in as the Transatlantic partners benefit from trade liberalization.

Black Swans and Forecasting Limitations

The result of a weaker Europe, slower growing emerging markets, and the multitude of trends and factors detailed above is this: in the short term, real U.S. GDP growth is anticipated to decrease from 2.4 percent in 2014 to 1.9 percent in 2015, then climb to 2.6 in 2016, according to the Federal Reserve's Central Tendency average published June 17, 2015.

The Economic Research Service calculated a U.S. GDP growth rate of 3.2 percent during the period 1971-1980, 3.36 percent during 1981-1990, 3.45 during 1991-2000, and 1.66 during the years 2001-2010. Moving forward, it predicts a 2.53 percent GDP rate during the period 2011-2020, and 2.6 during the years 2021-2030.

When forecasting future economic growth, the ability to do so accurately is extremely difficult. Assessing and understanding the impact of existing or known risks is very challenging, and it's virtually impossible to predict the economic impact of unforeseen risks and events in the future. The emergence of "black swans" don't help.

According to author Nassim Nicholas Taleb, a black swan, a term he coined, is a highly unlikely event that carries a massive impact. For example, on March 11, 2011, a black swan devastated Japan. It involved not one, but a series of highly unlikely events beginning with a violent earthquake and ending in a tsunami and a nuclear crisis. In addition to a tremendous loss of life and property, Japanese suppliers to the United States were paralyzed for months. In turn, many American supply chains broke down causing a harmful ripple effect through several industries. Who could have predicted that?

In addition, emotions often play a sizeable role in the direction of economic growth. They affect confidence — a key factor in determining the level at which consumers and businesses spend and invest money. Emotions are not rational and certainly not based on economic fundamentals, as often witnessed by the herd mentality that, when fear strikes, can cause vast swings in the stock market. Acts of terrorism, as seen through the 9/11 attacks, by design inflict fear, cause emotional distress, create insecurity, and quickly change behavior.

On the other hand, President Ronald Reagan, for example, understood the power of cheerleading and a positive attitude. From his earliest days as a public speaker to his final days in the public eye, Reagan consistently invoked America's greatness. Through his message that America was "a shining city on a hill" and that its promise was boundless, he inspired Americans and boosted their level of confidence.

Emotion and confidence, and the direction they take in an environment of quickly changing events, adds a significant but virtually impossible variable to identify in advance. As a result, accurately predicting short-term economic growth has its limitations. However, assessing long-term trends is another story.

Since the start of the world financial crisis, the longest downturn in U.S. postwar history has given way to a lackluster recovery. And there is no doubt that the United States will continue to experience economic difficulties and some black swans in the years ahead that will cause American capitalism to underperform. Nevertheless, due to America's "secret sauce," a subject covered later, I am optimistic about the long-term future of the United States.

U.S. PRODUCTION AND ABUNDANT ENERGY

When asked to describe the state of American manufacturing, many say it has been "hollowed out." When asked why, they point to the decline in manufacturing jobs, note the few "Made in America" products on retail store shelves, and identify importing and offshoring as the culprits. Although many of these reasons appear persuasive, they're not accurate.

THE TRUTH ABOUT AMERICAN MANUFACTURING

U.S. manufacturing employment, no doubt, has declined from a high of 19.5 million workers in 1979 to approximately 12 million today. The primary reason, however, has everything to do with technology, innovation and automation, which have empowered fewer employees to produce much more in less time. In turn, productivity in the manufacturing sector has been improving and increasing faster than productivity growth in other sectors of the U.S. economy.[1]

Another factor impacting the decline in manufacturing jobs is this: 30 to 55 percent of manufacturing jobs in advanced economies are in service-type functions.[2] As producers continue to focus on their core competencies and contract various functions to local suppliers, many positions in marketing, design, payroll, accounting, and human resources are shifted to local marketing, accounting, payroll and employment agencies, and no longer are classified in manufacturing statistics.

Surprising to many, manufacturing value-added output has not decreased. In fact, with the exception of recessionary periods, it has risen each year, jumping from $545 billion in 1979 to $2.1 trillion in 2014, the Bureau of Economic Analysis reports. When accounting for inflation, the story is the same. But what is occurring in the manufacturing sector already has occurred in the agricultural sector. According to the Bureau of Labor Statistics, in 1940, 9.5 million U.S. workers were employed on farms, but by 2014 this number had declined to approximately 2 million. Nonetheless, U.S. agricultural output skyrocketed.

When walking down the aisles of many retail stores, few products carry the "Made in America" label.

There's a good reason. Today, an increasing number of American manufacturers produce high margin, higher technology products that incorporate significant levels of intellectual property, such as medical equipment, pharmaceuticals, aerospace equipment, and computer chips, and no longer focus on consumer goods to the extent they did in the past. In turn, many consumer products are imported.

Numerous Americans believe imports are bad for the economy and hurt the manufacturing sector. One reason cited involves the negative impact of imports on GDP. Thus, in 2014 U.S. GDP was $17.4 trillion, according to the Bureau of Economic Analysis. One of the main line items, Net Exports of Goods and Services or the difference between exports and imports, was nearly -$538 billion. As a result, many draw the conclusion that imports are damaging to the economy. In reality, it's not that simple.

Imports offer American consumers greater choices, a wider range of quality, and access to lower-cost goods and services. They also create competition, forcing domestic producers to improve value by increasing quality and/or by reducing costs. Plus, since imports like inexpensive clothing allow the American family to purchase more goods for less money, stretching the dollar, more disposable income is available for other things, such as education and health care.

Imports also help keep inflation down, which is one of the most important factors in raising our standard of living. And since more than half of all U.S. imports are intermediate inputs used in the final production of U.S. products, they also help U.S. manufacturers remain globally competitive.

Of course, attractive imports that compete directly with U.S.-produced products do cause U.S. job dislocations. But also surprising to many, the number is much smaller than generally assumed. And even more surprising is the number of U.S. jobs created from imports. Research by the Heritage Foundation, a Washington, D.C.-based think tank, cites "the increased economic activity associated with every stage of the import process helps support American jobs. A lot of them."

For example, the Heritage Foundation says over half a million jobs are supported by imports of Chinese-made clothes and toys alone: "These are jobs in fields such as transportation, wholesale, retail, construction, and finance, and in a myriad of other activities that are involved in turning a manufactured product into a good that is ready for use by the average American."

Backshoring and the
Impact of Investing Abroad

When U.S. manufacturers decide to invest abroad, they typically are not seeking cheap labor. In fact, the cost of labor is only one of many factors considered. Other factors include the availability of skilled workers, productivity levels, the quality of local infrastructure, political stability, rule of law, proximity to key markets and supply chains, and the ability to repatriate profits. A more recent trend involves "nearshoring," where manufacturers move production and/or distribution facilities closer to fast-growing overseas markets in order to better serve consumers while reducing transportation costs.

Simply put, if cheap labor was the primary consideration when companies invest abroad, Haiti would be a manufacturing powerhouse — and the United States, which certainly does not offer cheap labor, would not be the top destination of the world's foreign investment.

Stated by Daniel Ikenson, Director of The Cato Institute's Herbert A. Stiefel Center for Trade Policy Studies, "As of 2013, nearly $1 trillion of foreign direct investment was parked in U.S. manufacturing, by far the number-one manufacturing investment destination world-wide. Clearly, the most successful foreign-headquartered companies see a future for U.S. manufacturing."

When U.S. manufacturers invest abroad, the impact on the United States also is very different than public opinion might suggest. In fact, U.S. multinationals that increase their investments abroad simultaneously increase the size and strength of their manufacturing activities in the United States.[3] This conclusion is based on data from U.S. manufacturing multinationals over a 20-year time period.

A typical example may resemble this: a U.S.-based manufacturer establishes a production facility in Brazil to support its expanding Latin American consumer markets. In turn, the U.S. affiliate likely will import various components from its U.S.-based facility, as well as its intellectual property. Consequently, the U.S.-based facility benefits.

Ralph Watkins, former trade analyst at the U.S. International Trade Commission and CEO of Americas Trade Analysis, LLC., notes that U.S. companies with manufacturing operations in China tend to contract out the supply of components to local producers in China and nearby suppliers in East Asia. The benefit to the Company's U.S. operation is limited.

When U.S. firms establish manufacturing facilities abroad, some plants in the United States may close as others open. However, data show that the creation of jobs abroad and the increase of sales abroad by U.S. multinationals are both associated with more jobs at home. And the statistics are impressive.

Thus, a 10 percent increase in employment at a foreign manufacturing affiliate is associated with an increase in its U.S.–based operation of 6.2 percent in research and development spending, 3.9 percent in sales, 3.8 percent in employment, and 3.8 percent in exports. Similarly, a 10 percent increase in sales at a foreign manufacturing affiliate is associated with an increase in its U.S.–based operation of 8.2 percent in research and development spending, 2.5 percent in sales, 2.2 percent in employment, and 2.6 percent in exports. And this does not include the increases experienced by U.S.-based service firms associated with the foreign based operation.[4]

For our partner to the south, the data indicate that for every 100 jobs U.S. manufacturers create in the Mexican manufacturing sector, they add nearly 250 jobs at their larger U.S. home operations, and also increase their U.S. research and development spending by 3 percent.[5] As one can see in the daily papers and on television, the misperceptions and myths surrounding the American manufacturing industry continue to perpetuate. The reality is quite different.

American manufacturing also will get a boost from backshoring or the returning of U.S. manufacturing activities from China and other developing countries back to the United States. In recent years, China has absorbed much of the United States' and the developed world's low-tech production. But if U.S. consumers are the primary market destination of this production, as opposed to Chinese or other Asian consumers, the Middle Kingdom may no longer be the attractive manufacturing location it once was.

For some time Chinese labor rates have increased by 15 to 20 percent annually due to a variety of factors, including a Chinese labor and skills shortage in coastal provinces, as well as the impact of China's appreciating currency, the renminbi. Plus, fuel costs and ever-increasing expenses related to global supply chain logistics and long distance management, along with capital outlays associated with longer lead times and larger inventories, have further reduced China's low-cost advantage. In addition, costs of engineers, purchasing managers and quality control staff traveling to China add up.

As a result, the wage gap between China and low-cost American states, such as Mississippi, South Carolina and Alabama has been reduced. In turn, the production of many goods that require less labor and are churned out in modest volumes have been shifting back to the United States and Mexico, while labor-intensive goods produced in high volumes will continue to be made abroad.

Consequently, many U.S. manufacturers producing lower technology goods in developing countries in order to access cheap labor are reworking the math. And due to improvements in automation, it may make sense to backshore or return previously offshored lower-tech manufacturing to the United States. The American energy revolution — another factor driving down U.S. costs — may accelerate backshoring.

Due to its proximity to the United States, Mexico, a low cost alternative, also is likely to become a beneficiary of backshoring. In the next few years, Cuba, with its low costs and relatively well-educated labor force, may also become a regional manufacturing destination. The bottom line: for U.S. producers interested in moving lower technology production abroad for the first time, it's worth a reevaluation of their global production and supply chain strategy.

The Impact of the American Energy Revolution

As the United States becomes an ever-greater energy producer, Russia, Saudi Arabia, Venezuela, and other relatively large energy producing countries will continue to be negatively impacted. And with decreasing U.S. dependency on Middle Eastern oil, China, the world's largest consumer of energy, will become more influential there. But the biggest impact will be on the United States, which stands to significantly benefit in terms of economic growth, manufacturing output and corporate competitiveness.

In 2013, the United States was the third largest global producer of crude oil after Russia and Saudi Arabia, and the world's biggest overall producer of oil. The U.S. also was the world's top producer of dry natural gas, followed by Russia, Canada and China.[6] As U.S. energy production increases, the impact will continue to be felt inside, as well as outside, the United States.

Several years ago, it was assumed that the United States would be importing increasingly larger volumes of petroleum and liquefied natural gas to make up for shortfalls in domestic production. However, with significantly greater energy output over the last few years, combined with greater automotive fuel efficiency, estimated net energy imports (imports minus exports), which peaked in 2005, continue to decline. In turn, the net import share of total U.S. consumption has been falling — from 30 percent in 2005 to 16 percent in 2012

— and is projected to decline further to 4 percent in 2040.[7]

In 2013, domestic energy production satisfied 84 percent of America's energy needs and included natural gas, which represented 30 percent of U.S. energy output. This was followed by coal, at 24 percent, petroleum, at 24 percent, renewables, at 11 percent, and nuclear power, at 10 percent.[8] Moving forward, natural gas will constitute a greater portion of domestically produced energy.

The combined use of horizontal drilling and hydraulic fracturing has enabled American companies to exploit untouched unconventional domestic energy resources such as shale gas, shale oil, and tight oil, all once considered too difficult to extract. In turn, due to improved recovery rates, assessments of these obtainable reserves have skyrocketed, even in already tapped fields.

It is estimated that reserves equivalent to those in the Persian Gulf may lie beneath North Dakota and Montana.[9] And the Marcellus shale alone may hold 141 trillion cubic feet of natural gas reserves, an amount equal to estimated world consumption in the year 2024.[10]

Technical developments in horizontal drilling allow vertical drilling systems to turn 90 degrees to steer in various directions well below the Earth's surface to reach areas not easily accessible. Hydraulic fracturing, also known as hydrofracking or fracking, is a process that injects mostly water, some sand, and chemical additives into the ground to create fissures in shale or other rock. In turn, shale gas is released and captured, while shale oil and tight oil seep back through the cracks and are extracted.

In the short term, this process is unlikely to be replicated in other areas of the world. The United States has an edge over other countries for a variety of reasons. These include the huge resource base of shale/tight oil existing in the United States, the nature of private ownership of mineral rights, the presence of thousands of independent drilling companies, large numbers of drilling rigs, and strong capital markets that fund new ventures.

As a result of new U.S. production, domestic natural gas output is projected to rise by 56 percent from 2012 through 2040, with production increasing to 37.6 trillion cubic feet annually.[11] Natural gas as a percentage of total U.S. energy production is projected to rise to 38 percent by 2040, followed by coal, at 23 percent, oil at 20 percent, renewables at 12 percent, and nuclear at 8 percent.[12]

A report card on the condition of America's infrastructure is released every four years by the American Society of Civil Engineers. The 2013 report card gave America's energy infrastructure a D+. An inadequate U.S. oil transportation system and refining infrastructure could slow energy progress.

According to the U.S. Chamber of Commerce's Institute for Twenty-First Century Energy, "U.S. oil pipelines could circle the equator eight times, and U.S. natural gas pipelines carry natural gas over 1.8 million miles each year." Nevertheless, the Institute says, "robust investments are needed to modernize, protect, and upgrade these critical assets, which are essential to America's national security, economic security, and way of life." Recent derailments of rail cars transporting crude petroleum from fields in Alberta, Canada and North Dakota to the Atlantic seaboard and refineries reinforce the need to invest in oil pipelines. But how much investment is required?

To deliver new gas supplies to existing pipelines that flow to the expanding American consumer market, it is estimated that 10,000 miles of new pipelines will be needed.[13] As reported in 2014 by Jennifer Dlouhy in the publication *Fuel Fix*, ICF International, a leading provider of consulting services and technology solutions, estimated that "companies will need to invest $641 billion over the next two decades just in pipelines, pumps and other infrastructure to keep up with the gas, crude oil and natural gas liquids flowing from U.S. fields." And that's not all.

According to Daniel Yergin, Vice Chairman of IHS, a research consulting company, the new light crude being recovered by hydraulic fracturing and horizontal drilling is a poor match for the refineries in the Midwest and along the Gulf Coast. These refineries, he says, have spent more than $100 billion in recent decades reconfiguring their equipment to process heavy, lower-quality imported oil from Canada, Mexico and Venezuela.

This puts considerable pressure on the private sector, which owns and manages more than 80 percent of our country's energy. But infrastructure shortfalls are only part of the problem. Environmental doubts about the safety of hydraulic fracturing from shale also could put the American energy revolution on hold. There have been more than one million hydraulic fracturing operations in the United States since 1947 and very few accidents have occurred.[14] Analysts say this risk can be managed by implementing best practices along with the enforcement of rules and regulations.

But a growing conflict between state and local governments and property owners (some governments have taken steps to prevent hydraulic fracturing and some property owners wish to sell their mineral rights) could result in lawsuits that could continue for years. Thus, during the summer of 2014, it was reported that five communities in Colorado voted to prohibit fracking, and more than 170 New York towns and cities used zoning laws to restrict it. In turn, this could slow the energy revolution.

The exploration and production of new American unconventional oil and natural gas, combined with related transportation, logistic and processing functions, is estimated to create nearly 2.9 million American jobs by 2015, 3.3 million by 2020, and approximately 3.9 million by 2025.[15] The value added contribution to GDP on an annual basis is tremendous, and estimated at approximately $400 billion in 2015, $470 billion in 2020, and $533 billion in 2025.[16] In addition, due to the reduction in natural gas prices, disposable income of American households is projected to increase from $2,700 in 2020 to $3,500 in 2025.[17]

Abundant low-cost American energy not only will benefit workers, households, and overall economic growth — it also will boost U.S. manufacturing output. A secure supply of low-cost natural gas will benefit many manufacturers, especially producers of iron and steel products, chemicals, plastics, resins, synthetic textiles and materials, and agricultural chemicals. And since gas-fired plants are an important source of electricity, lower electricity prices will benefit virtually every producer.

Due to a more competitive environment,

American manufacturing is projected to increase. This is anticipated on top of the backshoring trend. In turn, U.S. exports are projected to rise.

It is estimated that the United States will capture $70 to $115 billion in annual exports from other nations by the end of the decade. Surprising to many, approximately two-thirds of these export gains likely will come from the production shift to the U.S. from leading European nations and Japan.[18] Overall, by 2020, higher U.S. exports, combined with production that will likely be backshored from China, could generate 2.5 to 5 million American factory and service jobs associated with increased manufacturing.[19]

The recent dramatic decline in crude oil prices, not considered in the forecasts above, had brought costs down from a Cushing, Oklahoma West Texas Intermediate high 2014 spot price of $107.95 per barrel on June 20, 2014 to a low of $43.39 on March 17, 2015, the U.S. Energy Information Administration reported. Prior to this book going to print, the price had touched $61 in June 2015.

If sustained in the low $50s per barrel, the average U.S. family can save $750 in 2015, reports IHS Global Insight, a global market information and analytics company. Various factors play a role in the unexpected and precipitous drop in prices. Conspiracy theories

— including stories that the Saudis were attempting to crush the U.S. shale industry and that the U.S. was colluding with the Saudis to flood the market in order to bankrupt Russia — dominated the press.

Regardless of the reasons, world energy prices likely will rise. On the other hand, the U.S. domestic energy revolution resulting from horizontal drilling and hydraulic fracturing likely will keep prices down in the United States. U.S. energy flooding the domestic market will result in less American global demand. If this demand gap is not filled by China and other countries seeking greater energy imports, a plausible scenario, global energy prices will remain relatively low continuing to negatively impact energy exporters like Russia, Colombia, Venezuela, Angola, Nigeria, Iran, Iraq, and Saudi Arabia.

Russia, for example, which reportedly needs $110 per barrel to balance its budget, will have less global leverage since much of its economic strength is based on a high price of oil and gas. And if the United States should become a serious energy exporter (with minor exceptions, the United States banned exports of crude oil in the 1970s), more supplies worldwide would put Russia at a greater disadvantage.

Declining U.S. energy imports also translates into more money being spent in the United States on research and development, and wages and supplies, thereby benefiting local communities. This shift from imports to a more secure domestic supply also will, to some degree, shield the United States from future Middle East violence and volatility. On the downside, however, falling oil prices reduce the economic viability of alternative sources, such as wind and solar energy.

Since the 1970s, the United States Navy has and continues to be the lead provider of security in the sea lanes of the Persian Gulf, other Mideast waters, and the Indian Ocean. But in recent years, China surpassed the United States as the largest importer of crude oil from the Persian Gulf — a region estimated to hold 55 percent of conventional oil reserves. As American energy imports from the Middle East decline, and with it a degree of influence, China is likely to become a more influential player there as it becomes a larger buyer.

China also may attempt to patrol regional waters to a greater extent in an effort to secure its supplies. Stated by Yergin, "Some strategists in Beijing worry about China depending on a world oil market that they assert is unreliable, rigged against them, and in which the United States has, in their view, excessive influence. Some of them even argue that the United States has a strategy to interdict sea-borne Chinese oil imports —

cut off China's overseas 'oil lifeline' — in the event of a confrontation."

On the other hand, Yergin says some Americans strategists "argue that China, driven by a voracious appetite for resources and control, has a grand strategy to project its dominance over Asia while also seeking to preempt substantial world oil supplies." The bottom line: although the United States is becoming more energy secure, subsequent events could make the global environment more volatile.

GLOBALIZATION IS LIKE FIRE

I'm often asked if global economic integration or globalization is a positive or negative force. The answer is complex. Simply put, globalization is like a fire: it can keep you warm, cook your food, or burn your house down.

THE BENEFITS AND CHALLENGES OF GLOBAL ECONOMIC INTEGRATION

Globalization has had a tremendous impact on the world. On the upside, world poverty rapidly has fallen and globalization is largely responsible, according to Laurence Chandy and Geoffrey Gertz of the Brookings Institution, a Washington, D.C.-based public policy research organization.

In 2005, the World Bank estimated one in every four people in the developing world lived below the international poverty level of $1.25 a day. From 2005 through 2011, Chandy and Gertz say half a billion people escaped poverty. They estimate the poverty rate declined by approximately 70 million people each year, a number equal to the population of Turkey.

Chandy and Gertz credit a variety of factors that are all manifestations of global economic integration. And who would know this better than former Mexican president Ernesto Zedillo, who said, "In every case where a poor nation has significantly overcome its poverty, this has been achieved while engaging in production for export markets and opening itself to the influx of foreign goods, investment and technology — that is, by participating in globalization." The Brookings Institute says we are likely to see another 70 to 100 million people lifted out of extreme poverty in 2015.

Global engagement by American firms has produced some remarkable results. For example, on average, U.S. companies that export employ twice as many workers, produce twice as much output, and generally offer better health insurance and pensions than non-exporting companies, reports the Peterson Institute of International Economics. International trade also delivered approximately $1.7 trillion in benefits to the U.S. economy or $13,600 per American household in 2013.[1] Furthermore, according to the Business Roundtable, an association of chief executive officers of leading U.S. companies, trade accounts for nearly one in every five jobs.

Surprising to many, the American service sector is a tremendous exporter, generating a $232 billion trade surplus in 2014. This activity has supported millions of American jobs and continues to be a major source of economic growth.

When many people envision the service sector, however, they still think of employees flipping hamburgers in fast food restaurants. In reality, the U.S. service sector has become extremely advanced and internationally competitive. In turn, the sector's wages have risen considerably.

For example, in June 2015, average hourly earnings for service-providing employees reached $24.69, according to the Bureau of Labor Statistics. During this same month, average hourly earnings for U.S. manufacturing employees was $25.08. This indicates that hourly wages in the service sector have nearly caught up to the manufacturing sector.

With the introduction and availability of new and inexpensive technology — led by telecommunications, computers and the internet — millions of people and companies worldwide have the ability to purchase more services from the United States. In turn, tremendous benefits are derived from the service sector in terms of economic growth, personal income, employment and exports. This fact is not widely acknowledged.

Major U.S. service exports include computer and data processing; wholesale, financial, transportation and communication services; architectural, engineering and surveying services; accounting, research and management services; and motion pictures. It is anticipated that the export of business, professional and technical services (accounting, advertising, engineering, franchising, consulting, public relations, testing and training, and health care) will increase rapidly over the next several years.

This reality isn't just an American one. In developed nations, services represent approximately three-quarters of GDP. Even in China, the service sector represents about 50 percent of the economy.

International trade theory has its roots in the 18th century writings of Adam Smith. He argued that nations could increase their combined output if each specializes in producing goods for which it is most efficient, and then each engages in trade. Every country will be better off, he astutely claimed, in terms of the quantity of goods available for consumption, resources expended, and additional output obtained through specialization.

According to David Ricardo, a prominent classical economist, even if a nation does not possess an absolute advantage in the production of a commodity, it still will benefit by producing and exporting those products in which it has a comparative advantage. Put another way, the less efficient nation should specialize in and export the goods and services in which it has the least disadvantage. This personal contemporary example explains the point: if you can type letters faster than your assistant, who is paid considerably less than you, should you put aside your more sophisticated and profitable projects so you can type? No. You are better off delegating the typing to your assistant even though you are more proficient at it. In the end, 18th century trade theory still holds true.

Explaining the impact of specialization, Michael Licata, a senior economic development executive, tells the following story:

Each day, 10 fishermen ventured to the ocean to catch their family's food requirements. The task lasted all day. However, on one particular day, a fisherman brought a net he created by twining vines together. And in just six hours, he caught enough fish to supply all 10 families. Amazed, the other fishermen marveled over the new invention. One asked, 'What are you going to do with all that fish? Your family can't eat all of them. 'I guess you're right,' said the net man. 'I'll tell you what,' said another, 'I'll keep your roof from leaking if you give me enough fish to feed my family.' Another said, 'My wife has a garden, so I'll trade you vegetables for fish. And a third said, 'I hate fishing. If you catch my fish from now on, I'll hunt game and gather your firewood in the forest.' When the net man returned each day with his large catch of fish, he saw his wood chopped, vegetables near his door, and a brace of rabbits hanging on his fence. He even was able to sleep better since his roof no longer leaked during rainy nights. Others, too, benefited from various trades and ventured into other businesses. For example, one man learned to play an instrument he made out of wood and entertained villagers at night in exchange for goods and services. Another experimented with herbs and began curing certain illnesses. However, as specialization occurred and life improved for all 10 families, the fishing pole maker was not happy. His business worsened since fewer men now fished.

Just as in nature, if balance is lost, counter forces emerge that push back in an attempt to seek an arrangement that works. For example, when deer populations exceed their environmental limitations, dwindling food supplies reduce their number. This natural countering effect occurs in all systems, including religious, political and economic ones. For example, when overzealous popes wielded excessive power, the Protestant Reformation formed and challenged existing doctrine. When the Great Depression caused unemployment to skyrocket, Fascism emerged as an alternative political system. And, when unrestrained laissez-faire capitalism became the rage, Marxism provided the opposition.

Just as there was no halting the Industrial Revolution, global economic integration will not be stopped. But it can and has slowed during this last recession. The negative impact felt by globalization has much to do with the pace of change it creates. If companies and workers do not have enough time to adapt to changes posed by global economic integration, too much too fast can be debilitating. How fast is too fast is debatable.

Media coverage has not helped to provide a balanced perspective on global integration. Through misinformation and half-truths anti-globalist forces have persuaded tremendous numbers of people to fear, not embrace, global economic integration. And this is not new.

In December 1999, thousands of protesters disrupted the World Trade Organization meeting in Seattle. Police fired tear gas and rubber bullets on crowds of activists and the talks ended prematurely. In April 2000, thousands of protesters descended upon a World Bank and International Monetary Fund meeting paralyzing Washington, D.C. In September 2000, Czech police used tear gas and water cannons to prevent demonstrators from closing down a World Bank and International Monetary Fund conference in Prague. In April 2001, anti-globalization activists disrupted a Summit of the Americas meeting in Quebec, Canada. And in July 2001, young Italian activists were fatally shot by police in a confrontation at the G8 summit in Genoa, Italy.

Although anti-globalist voices have faded since the September 11, 2001 terrorist attacks on the United States, the movement remains strong. During the July 2005 G8 summit, 3,500 protesters, many shouting anti-globalization slogans marched through the Scottish village of Auchterarder near the Gleneagles Resort, the host of the summit. Several hundred protesters clashed with police.

Anti-globalist organizations, whose intentions are admirable, often describe themselves as human rights groups. In response, they achieve a moral high ground and, in turn, often get the benefit of the doubt from the press. Ironically, if the policies advocated by these organizations were ever implemented, they would do tremendous damage to the groups they seek to help.

During the 1970s and 1980s, Japan was the country most feared by the United States in terms of economic competition. In fact, in the minds of many, the promise of America was over; Japanese economic power would dictate. In the 1990s, Mexico became the focus of the American public. Ross Perot had millions of Americans convinced that we would all hear a "giant sucking sound" as U.S. jobs headed south, a famously incorrect forecast. Now, globalization and China are on the top of our minds in terms of economic threats. Is this justified?

As I noted earlier, the answer to the question of whether or not globalization is good certainly is complex. The answer is somewhat different for different groups.

For example, if a company's products are labor intensive or if an employee's skill base is limited, global economic integration, no doubt, will present an increasingly greater challenge. However, if a firm is focused on higher technology, intellectually rich products or if an employee's skill level is continually improved, the world will become an attractive market boosting the benefits of globalization. And for the United States overall, I believe this is the case.

Nevertheless, if a large number of Americans, including reporters, policymakers, employees and employers believe that global economic integration represents forces to fear, not opportunities to seize, successfully communicating the benefits of international engagement and open borders will require an even greater effort.

In 1950, international trade accounted for less than 5.5 percent of U.S. economic growth; today, it has become an integral part of everyday life, now contributing 30 percent. Those with higher skills tend to benefit the most from global engagement by being in a position to reap the greatest rewards from their products and services selling in world markets.

On the other hand, international competition has continued to increase here at home, putting greater pressure on American firms and workers to adjust. Yet, due to the accelerated pace at which change now occurs, many lower-tech industries have not been able to adapt and have gone out of business. And in some cases, not so low-tech industries have found it extremely difficult to compete against foreign industries that are unfairly subsidized or protected by their governments.

THE DANGERS OF CLOSING
ECONOMIES AND WHAT TO DO

The United States is one of the world's most open economies — and this has created many advantages here at home. The average U.S. import tariff on goods is less than 1.5 percent.[2] This is significantly lower than the average foreign country tariff of 5.9 percent.[3] However, various international organizations, including the World Trade Organization, United Nations, and the OECD recently have been sounding the alarm over what appears to be a sharp increase in protectionism around the world. These rising barriers to trade result, in part, in less global business, slower economic growth, and poor job gains. They also weaken the global economic recovery.

Barriers to trade are not new. They have been rising for some time. In the three years leading up to November 2011, countries have implemented 1,593 protectionist actions alone. India leads the pact of countries implementing the most protective measures targeted against the least developed countries.[4]

Over the past several decades, global tariff levels across the world have decreased. But as this has occurred, even though many countries are members of regional trade agreements, their governments have resorted to other forms of creative protectionism.

Known as non-tariff barriers to trade, they can include standards and regulations that discriminate against imported goods, quotas (limitations on import quantities), export performance requirements (the company importing the goods must export domestic goods of the same value), and government procurement preferences for domestically-made goods. Barriers also can include burdensome import documentation, licensing requirements, administrative entry procedures, and special supplementary duties and border taxes designed to protect domestic industries or stem the flow of foreign exchange.

To comply with Argentina's export performance requirements, for example, Daimler Benz purchased a winery in Argentina. In turn, the company uses foreign exchange earned by its exports of Argentine wine to offset the foreign exchange required to import auto parts used to assemble vehicles in Argentina. Alternative strategies for Daimler Benz would have been to manufacture the required auto parts in Argentina, export finished vehicles from Argentina, or close the assembly plant there.

Agricultural, land, financing, and corporate subsidies also can distort trade and unfairly provide a competitive advantage. And there are many other unfair trade practices not noted here. The bottom line: protectionism can have significant negative implications for domestic producers as well as foreign industries. By effectively preventing foreign competitors access to a domestic market, sheltered domestic producers tend to become complacent, producing costly, poor quality products inefficiently. This principle was exemplified by the industries of Eastern European nations during the reign of communism.

Examples closer to home include "buy American" programs that demand certain components or a specific minimum value be purchased in the domestic market. These programs, which generally are considered a tool to promote domestic employment, often cost more jobs than they create.

For example, the American Recovery and Reinvestment Act of 2009, better known as the $787 billion stimulus bill approved by Congress and signed into law by President Obama on February 17, 2009, included a buy American provision that essentially provided the ingredients to start a trade war. Although some exceptions existed, the buy American provision stated that all iron, steel and manufactured goods purchased by stimulus money must be produced in the United States.

According to a report published by the Peterson Institute for International Economics, the Senate version of the stimulus bill, which was adopted in the final bill, was expected to save or create 9,000 jobs. However, due to likely foreign retaliation and a resulting projected decrease in exports, the Peterson Institute concluded that the legislation would have cost more jobs than gained. The buy American provision was scrapped.

In another example, it was determined by Douglas

Irwin of the Cato Institutes that the buy American provision in the funding legislation for the rebuilding of the San Francisco-Oakland Bay Bridge in the 1990s would have cost California taxpayers $400 million more if the buy American provision had not been rescinded at the last minute. Overall, buy American provisions that restrict foreign supplies of steel or other products often have unintended consequences and typically do not achieve the intended results.

Unfortunately, some mistakes were not revealed until months after the offending legislation was implemented. For example, in December 2003, President George W. Bush announced his decision to remove steel tariffs he had imposed 21 months earlier. Nevertheless, the damage was done. U.S. steel users had incurred massive price increases as well as major supply disruptions, according to William Gaskin, President of the Precision Metalforming Association. The higher prices caused many steel-consuming industries to shrink. In the end, more jobs were lost than preserved by the restraint on imports.

Nearly a century ago, the United States learned harsh lessons from raising barriers. Although tariffs and quotas were designed to protect American industries and jobs from foreign competition, American protectionism triggered a wave of foreign barriers against U.S. exports and contributed to the Great Depression.

In the late 1920s, U.S. industrial production began to fall and U.S. farmers felt the effects of foreign agricultural competition. European agricultural recovery after World War I led to overproduction. As a result, international agricultural prices fell. The solution: on June 17, 1930, President Hoover signed the Smoot-Hawley Act that raised tariffs nearly 60 percent over their existing high rate of 44 percent. Although the act seemed like a good idea at the time, it effectively killed international trade. Within two years following the act's implementation, U.S. exports decreased by nearly two-thirds.

In anticipation of Smoot-Hawley's passage, France, Italy, India and Australia passed their own protectionist legislation. Others, such as Spain, Switzerland and Canada, followed suit. The result: export markets dried up and domestic industries slowed down. For the next eight years, international trade declined. The unemployment rate in the United States rose to 25 percent in 1933. What began as a sincere attempt to aid U.S. industry made an international crisis of the highest order more severe.

When used properly, trade barriers can be an important tool to keep dangerous products out of a country. For example, in 2007 it was widely reported that tainted food imports from China were making millions of Americans sick. That year, several types of farm seafood from China were suspended by the U.S. Food and Drug Administration after alarming quantities of an antibiotic were found in catfish, eel and shrimp, among other products. And that's not all. Chinese exports, from tires and toys to dog food, were found to have defects that endangered consumers.

Many other countries also were affected. Reports indicated that 100 people in Panama died after consuming cough syrup tainted with a Chinese-produced additive containing diethylene glycol, a component of car antifreeze. In turn, American regulators studied the situation and determined the toxin also was in U.S. imported toothpaste sold under discount brand names.

But it soon was determined that China wasn't the only country at fault. In fact, in just one month that year, the U.S. Food and Drug Administration rejected 1,322 imports from 75 countries that were determined to be tainted. Of these, 211 were from India, 185 were from mainland China, and 150 were from Mexico. And surprising to many observers, plenty of the rejected imports came from developed countries, including Canada, 39, and the United Kingdom, 37.

As more American importers investigated the

situation, it was found that with successive production runs, some low-cost country manufacturers had shifted to lower quality suppliers in order to cut costs, and did so without the knowledge of the contractor or buyer. Mattel, which years ago recalled millions of Chinese-made toys contaminated with lead paint, was one of the unsuspecting buyers. As a result, imports required constant attention then, and still do today. Those involved in the supply chain, in the United States or around the world, need to constantly monitor quality and where their components are sourced or be subject to legal liability should consumers be injured or sickened.

Regardless of the type of trade barriers erected or their usefulness, one thing is certain: trade barriers solely implemented to limit competition create winners and losers on a global scale. Large exporting companies have the resources to maneuver through often complex foreign import barriers, hire consultants or utilize in-house expertise to work through sometimes hidden trade barriers designed to keep competition out. Small companies typically don't. By eliminating confusing and unnecessary red tape through free trade agreements, small companies are put on a more level playing field and are better positioned to grow internationally.

Since the 1980s, I have witnessed American companies successfully compete anywhere in the world when the playing field is leveled — that is, when trade barriers designed to limit U.S. competition are eliminated. And the best way to achieve this is through the implementation of new and broader free trade agreements and other international deals designed to eliminate tariffs, reduce non-tariff barriers, and simplify import regulations.

How beneficial are free trade agreements? Surprising to many, the United States maintains a manufacturing trade surplus with its free trade agreement partners. This demonstrates that when the playing field is leveled, American firms can successfully compete and win. Nevertheless, a major problem exists. The United States currently only has 14 free trade agreements with 20 partners. However, the World Trade Organization indicates there are nearly 400 regional trade agreements around the world without U.S. participation. And the number of free trade agreements being implemented by our competitors is on the rise, giving them a competitive advantage over U.S. companies in those markets.

As a result, it is important for Congress to pass new agreements. But this is virtually impossible unless Congress continuously renews Trade Promotion Authority (TPA), also referred to as "Fast Track." First enacted in 1974, TPA requires Congress to pass or reject trade agreements without making any changes. Without

TPA, foreign governments are reluctant to make agreements and concessions that could be changed later by Congress.

As experienced in June 2015, TPA is a controversial topic but necessary to complete and ratify the Trans-Pacific Partnership (TPP) agreement between the United States and 11 other Pacific-bordering nations, and the Transatlantic Trade and Investment Partnership (TTIP) with the European Union.

The Trans-Pacific deal, which has been in negotiations for approximately five years, includes Australia, Brunei, Canada, Chile, Japan, Malaysia, Mexico, New Zealand, Peru, Singapore, the United States, and Vietnam. Together, these countries represent approximately 40 percent of global economic output and one-third of trade. The Trans-Pacific Partnership seeks to eliminate tariffs and non-tariff barriers to trade in goods, services, and agriculture, and to establish or expand rules on a number of issues, including intellectual property rights and foreign direct investment.

In addition, it "has the potential to harmonize existing agreements with U.S. FTA partners, attract new participants, and establish regional rules on new policy issues facing the global economy," the Congressional Research Service says. The Trans-Pacific negotiations also afford the opportunity to modernize the 20-year-old North American Free Trade Agreement. Plus, it can help the Obama Administration in its effort to "pivot to Asia" for the purpose of providing a counterweight to the rise of China.

The economic impact of the Trans-Pacific Partnership will depend on a number of factors, including the extent of trade liberalization achieved and the economic growth of member countries. Nevertheless, the Trans-Pacific Partnership would be the largest U.S. free trade agreement by trade flows, which reached $727 billion in U.S. goods exports to, and $882 billion in imports from Trans-Pacific Partnership countries in 2014.

Currently, the U.S. average tariff rate on foreign products is extremely low. What's more, 70 percent of products entering the U.S. pay no tariff at all. On the other hand, U.S. companies are faced with much higher tariffs when exporting to global markets, and exceptionally high tariffs on many of their products when exported to Trans-Pacific Partnership countries.

For example, according to the United States Trade Representative, tariffs in Trans-Pacific Partnership markets range up to 70 percent on automotive products, 35 percent on chemicals, 60 percent on building products, 75 percent on consumer goods, 25 percent on high-tech instruments, and 30 percent on health products, information and communications technologies. If these tariffs, as well as non-tariff barriers are removed, the Trans-Pacific Partnership, no doubt, will benefit American exporters.

But the greater gains may lie elsewhere. According to Ralph Watkins, CEO of Americas Trade Analysis, LLC., many U.S. products destined for Asian markets already are produced in Asia. As a result, the greater advantages are likely to come from U.S. exports of services, the strengthening of intellectual property rights, and the harmonization of standards and regulations, he says.

If an agreement on the Transatlantic Trade and Investment Partnership is concluded in its initial form, it will cover 50 percent of global output, 30 percent of world merchandise trade, and 20 percent of global investment, according to the OECD.

Although economic growth rates for the European Union are at historic lows, the world's largest trade bloc, which includes more than 500 million consumers compared with the U.S. population of 321 million, continues to have tremendous purchasing power. As a result, it remains a major market for U.S. exports. And since tariffs between the United States and European Union already are relatively low, the greater advantages may lie in the agreement's ability to effectively deal with agricultural export issues, intellectual property protection, access for U.S. services, and regulatory compliance.

Regulatory issues are considered key to a successful agreement, and include automobiles, chemicals, cosmetics, information communication technologies, medical devices, pesticides, and pharmaceuticals. According to the Congressional Research Service, "the two sides also seek to use eventual TTIP commitments on the global scene: to advance trade liberalization, set rules and standards; and address challenges associated with emerging markets."

As previously noted, the U.S. economy is increasingly driven by its service sector. Both the Trans-Pacific Partnership and the European deal strive to strengthen service sector exports — an essential factor in the future of American economic growth.

To achieve preferential trade agreements and ensure what's at stake is represented at the negotiating table, American companies must closely work with U.S. trade negotiators and provide up-to-date examples of foreign non-tariff barriers. Without new trade agreements enabling American firms competitive access to foreign markets, the backlash against global integration will continue to grow.

THE MIDDLE EAST'S REAL PROBLEM

Global economic integration or globalization often is cited as the cause of poverty in the Middle East. The opposite is actually true. A primary economic problem poor countries typically incur is not too much global economic integration, but rather, their lack of it. This, coupled with the absence of freedom, is a recipe for poor growth prospects, high unemployment, hopelessness and, ultimately, revolution. The disintegration of the Soviet Union illustrates the impact of economic isolation when combined with lack of freedom. Today, we are witnessing a similar phenomenon in the Middle East and North Africa.

Freedom House, an independent organization that supports the expansion of freedom around the world, says the Middle East and North Africa consistently register the worst civil liberties scores of any region. The region is full of totalitarian regimes that not only deny their citizens freedoms Americans cherish, but also use trade barriers to isolate themselves from the world, as well as from each other. As a result, the region's economy and unemployment levels are generally poor.

Regions or countries lacking economic and cultural connectivity with the rest of the world are those countries where you find instability, threats to the international system, and terrorist networks, says

Thomas Barnett, author of *The Pentagon's New Map*. On the other hand, economic integration and greater freedom in the Middle East and North Africa likely will have a major positive impact. The bottom line: no country has managed to lift itself out of poverty without integrating into the global economy. Why does global integration hold such promise for the Middle East and North Africa? Look at the facts.

For decades, East Asia and the Pacific, a region that has welcomed global integration, has generated annual growth rates among the highest in the world. If global integration is accepted in the Middle East and North Africa, the region will be positioned to absorb new ideas, technologies and a myriad of other benefits from the world trading community. This will help the region diversify its exports toward higher-value manufactured products, and in turn, create new jobs. Greater distribution of wealth will expand internal markets and create more employment opportunities.

As trade and investment increases, the incomes of ordinary people also will rise, creating a real middle class. This will lead to higher standards of living and a better-educated and politically involved population. Despair and hopelessness will slowly turn to hope, and those who were angry and disenfranchised are more likely to strap on money belts than bombs. The goal of ultimately establishing true capitalism and democracy in the Middle East will, no doubt, be difficult to achieve. But global economic integration helps.

WHAT WE CAN LEARN FROM DEMOGRAPHIC TRENDS

As the global economy continues to evolve, world populations continue to shift at a rate faster than ever. As a result, an understanding of demographic trends can help a company determine where to establish a production facility, sales office, warehouse or other investment. Population demographics also can determine the likelihood of civil strife, and economic and political instability.

When identifying the most lucrative markets around the world, companies often focus on a variety of demographic data, including disposable income, median age, mobility factors, home ownership, unemployment rates, and population trends. One of the most important factors, population growth, can be telling. A rising population often reflects a growing consumer base, and in turn, stronger demand. But for many countries, a population reversal currently is underway.

According to the U.S. Census Bureau, from 2014 through 2025, the population in Russia is projected to drop from 142 to 140 million; in Japan, from 127 to 123 million; and in Germany, from 81 to 79 million. What is the impact? Although these decreases appear small, they put economic growth at risk since the number of consumers, as well as those contributing value-added output, decreases.

Unlike many developed countries, noted earlier, the population of the United States is projected to increase from 321 million in 2015 to more than 346 million by 2025, according to the U.S. Census Bureau. Much of this growth is due to America's ability to attract immigrants, including the brightest from around the world. But what happens when a country's population grows too quickly — and when does this become a liability?

Edward Gresser, Executive Director of the Progressive Economy Project of the Global Works Foundation, a Washington, D.C.-based think tank, says the populations of South Asia, Africa, and the Middle East are surging. "Together they will likely add 1.7 billion new people by 2050 or three-quarters of all world population growth," he estimates. In countries with limited resources and environmental concerns, a rising population that puts too much pressure on an already-poor infrastructure can create tremendous problems.

What's more, the population of less developed countries with children under age 15 accounts for 28 percent of the population. Young persons, age 15 to 24, bring that total to 46 percent. As a result, the numbers of children and young people in the less developed regions are at an all-time high, posing a major challenge for their countries, the United Nations reports.

The situation in the least developed countries — which have the fastest growing populations in the world — is even more pressing. Children under age 15 constitute 40 percent of the population, and those age 15 to 24 bring that to 60 percent. This puts increasing pressure on educational institutions often competing for limited resources. But more importantly, if jobs are not created at a pace that effectively absorbs the flow of first-time entrants into the labor force, a quickly rising unemployment rate — often disproportionately borne by the youth — can result in civil strife or worse.

Not surprisingly, those countries with the highest fertility rates are among the poorest African countries. They also are the least likely to cope.

Fast-increasing young populations are not the only problem many developing countries face. Aging also is an issue. In the less developed regions, the population aged 60 and over is increasing "at the fastest pace ever — 3.7 percent annually in the period 2010-2015 and is projected to increase by 2.9 percent annually through 2050," the United Nations says. This adds pressure on younger workers to support an ever-increasing number of retirees.

Overall, the world's median age is rising and projected to increase from nearly 30 in 2015 to 36 by 2050. That means half the world's population will be younger and half older than 36. Broken down, by 2015, Germany is projected to have the world's highest median age of 46.5; Japan will follow in second place at 46.4. The United States will be in 52nd place with a median age of with 37.3. China, at 36.2; Brazil at 31.3; Mexico at 28.3; and India at 26.6 are projected to have younger populations. What does this mean for marketers?

Countries with higher median ages, which are typical of developed countries, generally have higher per capita incomes than their counterparts in developing countries. And in terms of products and services, pharmaceuticals and health-related products, for example, are more likely to be in greater demand, while producers of electronic games are more likely to discover stronger markets in countries with lower median ages.

But as noted above, countries and regions with very young and fast-growing poor populations — like Africa and Western Asia (including the Middle East), which in 2015 have median ages of nearly 20 and 27 — are a real concern. Unless significant job creation can be achieved and greater resources devoted to infrastructure improvements, an unlikely scenario, these young populations are likely to exacerbate tensions and cause unrest. In turn, increasing pressure placed on governments to improve economic conditions can escalate political risks.

CURRENCY ASSUMPTIONS ARE NO LONGER VALID

Since August 2011, the value of the U.S. dollar has continued to rise. In the past, a strengthening dollar meant imported sweaters from Bangladesh, for example, would be cheaper. In turn, it was anticipated that American retailers would buy more of them, boosting the trade deficit. On the export side, a rising dollar was a curse for an American producer, whose overseas prices would go up, pushing sales down. But today, the impact isn't so clear.

In 2014, $1.26 trillion or 54 percent of all U.S. imports were not consumer goods from low cost countries, but imports of industrial supplies and materials ($665.5 billion) and capital goods ($591.4 billion), the Bureau of Economic Analysis reports. These sources of supply are used by American manufacturers to improve their products and make them more globally competitive.

A rising dollar reduces the import price of these industrial supplies, materials, and capital goods. When used in production or assembly with domestically-sourced American goods for export, the lower cost of imported supplies often neutralizes the higher export price of domestic materials and components.

This scenario is more common than many may think. Today, a company's production and supply chains may stretch across the globe, connecting with dozens of other producers and suppliers. As a result, it's not unusual for a California-based company to receive industrial supplies and materials from several Asian and Latin American firms, and in turn, incorporate the materials into products that are ultimately shipped to Canadian and European customers.

Consequently, the sophistication and complexity of today's supply chains often mean more components and materials switch hands and incur value-added processes in different countries on their way to the final buyer. This process is quite different from the days when a product was entirely produced in one country, utilizing all domestic inputs, and exported to another.

In addition to this web of co-production across borders, other factors play a greater role that, in turn, have made previous currency assumptions invalid. These include a decline in the pass-through rate, the availability of domestic and foreign substitutes, and the opportunity costs of finding new suppliers.

If, for example, the Chinese renminbi rises by 3 percent relative to the U.S. dollar, and Chinese exports to the United States also rise by 3 percent, the pass-through rate would be 100 percent. But today, exporters often are willing to reduce the pass-through rate to preserve foreign market share. This being the case, a Chinese exporter may reduce his margins to neutralize the appreciation of the renminbi so the final price to American customers remains the same. This, no doubt, has an impact on old black and white currency assumptions.

Over the past few decades, the value of the dollar has incurred a roller coaster-like ride. In March 1973, the Federal Reserve's Nominal Major Currencies Dollar Index, a weighted average of foreign exchange values of the U.S. dollar against a number of currencies, was set at 100. It reached a high of 143.9 in March 1985, and fell to an all-time low of 69.0 in August 2011. Since then it generally has continued to rise reaching 91.67 in March 2015 and 89.7 in June 2015, just before this book went to press.

Years ago when the dollar was declining in value, the general assumption anticipated higher priced imports, and in turn, a reduction in the trade deficit. But this did not occur.

Between 2002 and 2005, the U.S. dollar depreciated 23 percent against the Canadian dollar and 24 percent against the euro, says Daniel Ikenson, Director of The Cato Institute's Herbert A. Stiefel Center for Trade Policy Studies. However, during this period, the U.S. trade deficit with Canada and members of the Eurozone rose by 58 and 39 percent, respectively.

Ikenson reported that of the other major U.S. trading partners, including Japan, the United Kingdom, South Korea, Taiwan, and Brazil, whose currencies appreciated against the dollar during the same 2002-2005 period, only Taiwan's trade surplus with the U.S. declined — but only by a modest 8 percent. And this was primarily due to more Taiwanese producers shifting the assembly of consumer goods, including bicycles, furniture, and laptop computers, to China, says Ralph Watkins, CEO of the research firm Americas Trade Analysis, LLC. In contrast, the U.S. deficit increased by 18 percent with Japan, 22 percent with Korea, 71 percent with the United Kingdom, and 181 percent with Brazil.

Many believe today that if China were to allow its currency to float, it would strengthen against the dollar making U.S. imports from China more expensive, and in turn, would reduce the mounting U.S.-China trade deficit. These assumptions are no longer valid.

In July 2005, when China reportedly pegged its exchange rate to a fixed basket of currencies, one U.S. dollar could buy 8.28 renminbi. Years later in early

July 2015, one dollar could only buy about 6, reflecting a stronger Chinese currency. Nevertheless, during this period the U.S.-Chinese trade deficit has continued to climb.

The belief that China's currency will rise if allowed to float doesn't consider China's current economic problems. In fact, if allowed to float, it may become volatile and decline in value due to China's current financial issues and modest economic growth, as compared to its stellar double-digit growth in recent years. And even if Chinese exports to the U.S. were somehow limited, U.S. importers would seek out other foreign suppliers of low-cost goods likely resulting in a still-large U.S. trade deficit. Interestingly, the composition of exports from China is becoming more technology oriented as brand name marketers shift the sourcing of labor-intensive products such as shoes, clothes, and furniture to Vietnam, Cambodia, and other countries with lower labor costs, Watkins says.

The bottom line: the rising or weakening dollar doesn't necessarily have the same impact it once did. As a result, old assumptions need to be reevaluated to account for today's dynamic trade patterns.

Another consideration impacting the strength of the dollar is whether or not it will continue to be the world's primary currency. As the European Union continues to struggle with economic difficulties, it has become increasingly clear that the euro is unlikely to significantly gain in stature against the dollar any time soon. In fact, some analysts are questioning the euro's future and asking how a union of different economies, fiscal disciplines, democracies, histories, values and languages could all use a common currency without encountering serious problems.

Some believe the Chinese renminbi eventually could gain in stature to challenge the dollar for world dominance. Nevertheless, in the next several decades, it is doubtful the greenback will fall from first place, a position it's held since usurping the British pound after World War I.

Understanding the impact of these factors, as well as the knowledge that fluctuations in the value of the dollar could have very different consequences than even a few years ago, can improve the decision-making abilities of companies, while reducing risk. Importantly, there are very serious implications for policymakers, who may implement poor policies based on old assumptions.

CHAPTER SIX

THE NORTH
AMERICAN BLOC

In order to strengthen free world economies and help contain the spread of former Soviet communism after World War II, the United States encouraged allied countries to export to the United States with few restrictions. This policy accelerated the economic recovery of postwar Europe and East Asia, ignited export-led growth in many developing countries, and helped revive international capital flows and promote global integration.

Consumers found that the market system could produce and distribute goods at affordable prices, where state planning could not. Consequently, the success of the free markets exposed the failures of the former Soviet communist system and scored impressive U.S. foreign policy victories.

In many cases, however, this policy sacrificed U.S. industries due to non-reciprocation from trade partners. Where the United States eliminated trade barriers, trading partners did not, putting U.S. firms at a disadvantage. At the time these problems were given little attention due to continued strong U.S. economic performance and greater priority given to the U.S. State Department over the Commerce Department. Consequently, trade policy often became an instrument of foreign policy.

With its huge internal market, the United States served as the locomotive for the world economy. By stimulating U.S. domestic demand, the United States was able to ward off global depression. But as the global political situation changed, so did the focus of the U.S. government. In the years ahead, American trade policy would serve U.S. companies and workers.

THE NAFTA RESULTS ARE IN... FINALLY

The year 1965 was a seminal year for North American trade and industrial integration. That year, the United States and Canada signed the Automotive Products Trade Agreement (APTA), allowing for the free flow of auto parts and assembled vehicles between the two countries. APTA was very successful and served as the template for the U.S.-Canada Free Trade Agreement, which was implemented in 1989. Also in 1965, Mexico opened its border region, then later the rest of the country, to foreign investment in export-oriented assembly plants.

The Mexican Maquiladora Program allowed companies to import parts and other manufacturing inputs free of duty provided that the assembled goods were exported and not sold in Mexico. Together, APTA and the Maquiladora Program planted the seed for the North American Free Trade Agreement (NAFTA), which bore fruit three decades later.

In January 1990, Mexican President Carlos Salinas de Gortari visited Europe to promote foreign investment that would support the Mexican trade liberalization process and serve as a counter-weight to the U.S.-Canada Free Trade Agreement. He found the Europeans preoccupied with Eastern Europe. It became apparent that Europe would not be a sufficient source of investment or destination for Mexico's exports. Mexico would have to depend upon U.S. investment and markets to increase productivity, exports and wages.

Through a U.S.-Mexico free trade agreement, President Salinas hoped to stimulate Mexican economic growth by increasing trade and investment. President Salinas also saw that a free trade agreement would likely prevent future Mexican presidents from deviating from his economic policies which he believed were essential to provide the stability necessary to promote long-term economic growth.

From Mexico's perspective, the anticipated benefits of greater economic integration included increased and secure access to the U.S. market; achievement of international credibility and a gain of foreign investment; improved domestic confidence in Mexico's economic future and the return of flight capital; access to U.S. technology and expertise; the development of economies of scale; higher productivity; a movement toward greater specialization; an increase in jobs and wages resulting in a higher standard of living with a more equal income distribution; improvement of working conditions; and a reduction in the so called brain drain or loss of educated workers through migration.

Presidents George H. Bush and Salinas defined a U.S.-Mexican free trade agreement as a process of gradual and comprehensive elimination of trade barriers between the United States and Mexico, including the full, phased elimination of import tariffs; the elimination or fullest possible reduction of non-tariff trade barriers, such as import quotas, licenses and technical barriers to trade; the establishment of clear, binding protection for intellectual property rights; fair and expeditious dispute settlement procedures; and other means to improve and expand the flow of goods, services and investment between the United States and Mexico.

President Salinas was successful in persuading U.S. President George H. Bush to enter into bilateral free trade negotiations. Canada later joined in the negotiations.

From Canada's perspective, the expected benefits of NAFTA included better access to Mexico's large and growing market; establishment of guarantees protecting intellectual property rights; enhanced competitiveness at home and abroad; establishment of long-term guarantees protecting Canadian direct foreign investment; the development of economies of scale; greater productivity; a movement toward greater specialization; and availability of less-expensive products. (Note: NAFTA incorporated the benefits Canada already had derived from the U.S.-Canada Free Trade Agreement.)

The United States had several fundamental objectives in pursuing a free trade agreement with Canada and Mexico. These included increasing U.S. exports to Mexico, thereby growing the number of well-paying U.S. jobs; the continued pursuit of Mexican trade and investment reforms, especially intellectual property rights, which would generate substantial new opportunities for U.S. firms; more efficient uses of natural and human resources in North America, in turn promoting U.S. world competitiveness; and Mexican economic growth and prosperity, increasing the Mexican standard of living and reducing the number of undocumented Mexican immigrants in the United States.

What are the results of NAFTA?

Unfortunately, NAFTA has become one of the most misunderstood trade agreements in history. Due to a massive dissemination of misinformation by anti-NAFTA interests, including Ross Perot back in the early 1990s, a large segment of the U.S. population continues to believe that NAFTA is not in the interest of the United States, and has accelerated the loss of U.S. jobs and a decline in U.S. wages. Ironically, through NAFTA, the exact opposite has occurred.

Unfortunately, organized labor has continued to perpetuate its counter-factual anti-trade myths in opposing agreements with Central America, Panama, Colombia, the Pacific Basin, and Europe.

U.S.-CANADIAN ECONOMIC INTEGRATION

In 2014, $658 billion worth of goods crossed the U.S.-Canada border. And that doesn't include trade in services. As a result, Canada, with a population of 35 million, continues to be the United States' largest trading partner responsible for 16.6 percent of all U.S. trade. What's more, Canada is the biggest merchandise export market for the majority of American states.

For a variety of reasons, Canada's financial system and housing market remain relatively strong and did not incur the same problems experienced in the United States due to the Great Recession. And during the period shortly after 2008, China's demand for Canada's considerable mineral, energy and agricultural resources helped our northern neighbor remain resilient against declining U.S. demand.

Canadian Prime Minister Stephen Harper once said, "Canada and the United States are staunch allies, vital economic partners, and steadfast friends." I couldn't agree more. Evolving from the U.S.-Canada Auto Pact into the U.S.-Canada Free Trade Agreement, and finally, into NAFTA, these accords have eliminated barriers to trade, investment and the movement of people across our shared border. In turn, this has greatly advanced north-south integration, stimulated the development of sophisticated supply chains and boosted bilateral trade. But that's not all.

Economic integration also has boosted capital flows, enhanced productivity, advanced the spread of technology, increased the number of product choices while keeping prices low for consumers, created more good-paying jobs, and elevated North American competitiveness. In this new and dynamic global business environment, the United States and Canada don't just make goods for each other. We make goods together for world markets. Consequently, it's not uncommon for a product to begin its manufacturing process in the United States, be shipped to a plant in Canada where valuable components are added and tested, be trucked back to a U.S. facility for completion and packaging, then be exported to a European buyer.

To ensure expeditious passage across the U.S.-Canada 5,525 mile-long border, a vital factor impacting supply chain efficiencies, corporations on both sides of the border continue to satisfy requirements and participate in voluntary security programs. This is extremely important since border delays drive up costs, drive down productivity, and shift just-in-time delivery to just-in-case procedures that demand larger, more expensive inventory stockpiles.

Surprising to many, the cumulative expenditures of delays are enormous. For example, several years ago analysts estimated it cost $800,000 for every additional hour of inventory to cover the risk of shipment disruptions of American parts headed to Canadian plants. Additional costs include wasted fuel in idling trucks, additional drivers to satisfy stringent trucking hours and service requirements, and extra trucks to account for those waiting in line. But this is only part of an emerging problem. If, for example, it becomes cheaper to ship Chinese automobiles east to Canada than to truck American automobiles north, other issues are sure to emerge.

Western New York, my home region, plays a vital role in streamlining U.S.-Canadian trade while enhancing North American competitiveness. Numerous studies indicate that Western New York is a prime location for a world-recognized logistics and distribution hub — which currently is in the works. Based on projected trade patterns and the region's assets and strategic advantages, this is anticipated to generate long-term sustainable economic growth and create well-paying jobs in Western New York far into the future.

Logistics centers typically concentrate regional product distribution, consolidate activity, improve carrier efficiency and reliability, and reduce inventory and supply chain costs. Yet, due to Western New York's proximity to Canada, a major logistics and distribution hub could provide a great deal more.

Improvements in regional transportation infrastructure and expansion of an international gateway connecting Western New York to Ontario would alleviate traffic delays, streamline the movement of goods and services, and improve efficiencies — major factors driving down operational and supply chain costs. This would enable the U.S. and Canada to further integrate manufacturing and services activities, and in turn, promote the spread of technology, as well as further boost innovation, productivity and North American competitiveness. Importantly, located within a short distance of Hamilton, Canada's prime manufacturing center, and Greater Toronto, Canada's largest consumer market, a Western New York logistics and distribution hub would be within a one-day 500 mile drive to over half of Canada's and America's total populations.

Since the completion of the Erie Canal in 1825, the Western New York region has evolved into a cluster of international logistics industries, including customs brokers, freight forwarders, logistics firms, warehousing and fulfillment operations, and government agencies that promote and regulate trade. In addition, law, accounting and consulting firms have developed expertise in immigration, customs, international accounting, business and marketing. Plus, the region's transportation infrastructure has grown to include major railroads and international bridge crossings, an extensive federal and state highway system, two international airports and one port.

Studies indicate that greater benefits exist when

adding value to products near the point where they change modes of transportation. As a result, Western New York's tremendous assets could further be developed to support light manufacturing and assembly operations, and to a greater extent, incorporate the benefits of foreign trade zones, effectively functioning as a sophisticated "northern Maquiladora." If marketed, branded and developed correctly, a world-recognized logistics and distribution hub could become extremely attractive to domestic and foreign investors interested in making one investment to serve two countries.

THE DIRECTION OF THE
U.S.-MEXICAN PARTNERSHIP

In 2014, the United States exported merchandise to Mexico valued at $240 billion, nearly the same amount as U.S. exports to China, Germany, the United Kingdom and Russia combined. This surprises many since Mexico, the second largest U.S. export market, has an economy less than one-tenth the size of the United States' and its population of 122 million is the world's 11th largest. But the benefits don't end there. On average, each Mexican consumed nearly $2,000 of U.S. goods in 2014. In comparison, on average, each Chinese citizen spent about $90 on American goods.

NAFTA, implemented more than 20 years ago,

was an important step in the continuing integration of the North American manufacturing base and the strengthening of the U.S.-Mexican partnership, enhancing the region's global competitiveness. According to Carla Hills, former U.S. Trade Representative, about half of our trade with Mexico takes place between related companies. As with Canada, we simply don't just make goods for each other, we make goods together for world markets. Consequently several U.S. and Mexican industries have come to rely on each other, contributing to a rich North American supply chain.

Mexico is the United States' third largest supplier. Interestingly, "a full 40 percent of the content of U.S. imports from Mexico was originally made in the United States, and it is likely that the domestic content in Mexican imports from the United States is also very high," according to the Woodrow Wilson International Center for Scholars in Washington, D.C. In comparison, 4, 3, and 2 percent of U.S. imports from China, Brazil and India, respectively, are comprised of U.S. origin content, the Center notes.

"The integration of the United States and Mexican economies has transformed the nature of the bilateral relationship from one of competition to partnership. U.S. jobs, competitiveness and economic growth all have benefited from the nation's relationship with Mexico," the Woodrow Wilson International Center says.

The U.S.-Mexican trade relationship has an extensive and rich background. Beginning in World War II, Mexican workers were invited to the United States to harvest crops under the Bracero program. And as early as 1965, U.S. manufacturers had established relatively easy access to inexpensive Mexican labor under various programs that enabled U.S. firms to co-produce in Mexico, and then ship goods back to the United States incurring very low duties. Although NAFTA provided significant benefits when it took effect on January 1, 1994, American companies already had become very familiar with the Mexican landscape.

Much of Mexico's ability to attract investment lies in its relationship with the United States. Privileged access under NAFTA and its proximity to the U.S. has given Mexico an edge in the production of automotive, heavy manufacturing and other industries where low transport costs and just-in-time logistics are crucial to competitiveness. During the 2000 to 2005 period, China began to encroach upon Mexico's share of the U.S. market. Since then, however, Mexico has been able to maintain its market share, says Ralph Watkins, CEO of Americas Trade Analysis, LLC.

Compared with China, Watkins reports, key

elements contributing to Mexico's level of competitiveness involve the proximity of Mexican assembly plants to American facilities located on the U.S. side of the border. This contributes to lower transportation costs, less time from manufacture to market, easier communication and supervision of production, and greater flexibility for changes in production. Importantly, Watkins says additional factors also give Mexico a leg up over China. These include more transparent government regulations and better intellectual property protection. Overall, Watkins says Mexico has an advantage over China when U.S. companies require just-in-time delivery, customized production and frequent design changes.

Mexico is becoming a beneficiary of U.S. backshoring, which involves American companies relocating previously offshored production back to the United States from China and other developing countries due to rising costs abroad. This is anticipated to further boost U.S.-Mexican trade in the years ahead.

The International Monetary Fund indicated that Mexico's GDP growth reached 2.1 percent in 2014, and is projected to reach 2.4 percent in 2015 and 3 percent in 2016. These estimates are higher than those projected for Latin America as a whole, but not as high as the rates projected by the International Monetary Fund for emerging markets and developing economies moving forward.

In some cases, analysts indicate that foreign direct investment destined for Mexico has been curtailed due to fear of Mexico's ongoing drug war. Mexico's ability to gain greater control of events in this illegal and violent sector will certainly impact both inbound investment and tourism for years to come.

In an attempt to improve his country's economic performance and level of global competitiveness, Mexican President Enrique Peña Nieto has embarked on an ambitious reform agenda that includes many sectors, including energy, education, telecommunications, financial services, labor, and fiscal issues. In the long term, the level of success achieved by these reforms will not only impact Mexico, but North America as well.

THE FUTURE OF A U.S.-CHINA DOMINATED WORLD

In the coming years, no relationship will have as much impact on America, our businesses, our children, and the world as the United States-China relationship.

China continues to offer American firms tremendous opportunities. However, at the same time, greater competition, new risks, political tensions, and misperceptions have emerged that are altering the relationship to a degree. In the years ahead, these factors will play out creating new challenges. Understanding these challenges and their impact will be crucial.

CHINA IN TRANSITION

China achieved double digit growth rates for decades. And in the last 30 years, the country lifted 500 million people out of poverty, according to the World Bank. Today, China is the world's largest manufacturer and exporter, and the second largest economy measured in gross domestic product or GDP. Its future, however, is not so clear.

In the coming years, the Middle Kingdom must overcome tremendous challenges that may significantly impact its competitiveness and social stability. Stated by former World Bank Group President Robert Zoellick, "China has now reached a turning point in its development path. Managing the transition from a middle-income to a high-income country will prove challenging."

China continues to subscribe to many of the same economic policies and has exemplified various behaviors that other Asian nations embraced early in their development. In the short term, these policies led to strong economic growth in Japan, South Korea and Taiwan. But over time, flaws emerged that proved damaging. For example, at first these Asian nations effectively discouraged individual consumption due to poor or non-existent safety nets and channeled savings into selected industries protected from international competition.

In addition, government subsidies, which diverted resources away from potentially more efficient enterprises, and low bank lending rates, which were offered to favored industries and state-owned enterprises, often came at the expense of productivity. Plus, over time, government capital investment returned declining output. The lack of effective checks and balances created levels of corruption that were difficult to curtail. China has not been exempt from these problems. In fact, the Chinese consider corruption one of the biggest challenges they face. Yet this is only one of several issues negatively affecting China's overall performance.

Michael Novak, the author of dozens of books on the philosophy and theology of culture, stresses that checks and balances are to the political order what competition is to capitalism. China does not have a system of checks and balances, nor one that promotes competition. As a result, China's brand of one-party capitalism is undergoing difficulties that are likely to increase. With an understanding of the problems ahead, in November 2013, Chinese President Xi Jinping released his first economic blueprint.

It called for market forces to play a larger role in the economy, along with many other reforms. And reported more recently, the Chinese leadership continues to pressure state-owned enterprises to rely less on state subsidies and more on the market. But with lower projected economic growth ahead, this option is less likely to become a reality in the near future. In the same blueprint, analysts note many contradictions and anticipate little or no real improvement in political reform in the near term.

To a major extent, the state rather than the market determines economic outcomes. And Chinese state-owned enterprises, reported by the Chinese Ministry of Finance to number more than 100,000 with assets of approximately $13 trillion, have provided much of this control. They also massively exceed the revenue of private Chinese companies. Because the state and its companies typically use capital less efficiently than private firms, a number of problems have emerged.

According to the Paulson Institute, a think tank with offices in the United States and China, "the returns of state-owned enterprises have sharply deteriorated. As a result, a significant part of the Chinese economy is underperforming. This creates a drag on economic output at a time when many other changes — an aging population, the maturing of housing and other infrastructure, and weak demand in the developed economies — are already shifting China onto a slower growth trajectory."

Surprising to many reformists who were hopeful that President Xi Jinping would make significant changes early in his tenure, Chinese reliance on state-owned enterprises is likely to continue. In November 2013 during the Third Plenum of the 18th Chinese Communist Party Central Committee, the leadership reiterated that state ownership continues to be a "pillar" and "foundation" of China's system. Although this pillar may be cracking, this statement is likely to remain true for some time.

Many other problems exist. China's one-child policy introduced in 1979 to alleviate social, economic, and environmental problems now is causing many unintended consequences. And the recent relaxation of the law is unlikely to undo demographic problems ahead. Reported in *The Wall Street Journal*, the United Nations Population Division indicates that each successive Chinese generation will shrink by 25 percent. Consequently, a decreasing workforce will be required to support an increasingly elderly population.

According to the International Monetary Fund 2013 working paper, "China is on the eve of a demographic shift that will have profound consequences on its economic and social landscape. Within a few years the working age population will reach a historical peak, and then begin a precipitous decline." But that peak may already have been reached. From 2011 to 2012, China's working population, age 15 to 59, declined by 3.45 million to 937.27 million, says *China Daily,* a leading English-language news organization in China. Ma Jiantang, head of the Chinese National Bureau of Statistics, says the working age population will steadily shrink. But the labor shortage may be influenced by other factors as well.

High real estate prices have pushed urban rental costs to the point where many workers simply can't afford to move to the cities where most factories are located. In turn, competition for Chinese labor, especially for work requiring higher skills, have driven up labor rates annually by double digits. An additional factor pushing rates even higher is the slow appreciation of China's currency.

"Wage increases can be a healthy sign of economic development, but China's is an unusual case," says Yonh Siew Wah, a Singapore-based consultant. "Whereas wages typically rise in line with worker productivity — employers will pay more for employees who are able to produce more — China's wage growth is mainly the result of government policies aimed at quickly increasing household income. Wage growth is far outstripping annual productivity increases." These factors are making China a less attractive manufacturing location for American firms primarily interested in supplying North American markets.

Falling birth rates and a shrinking workforce are not just China's problem; many European countries, including Russia, are experiencing similar situations. This, however, is not a problem in the United States, which has a growing population partially due to immigration. An expanding population, which typically reflects an increase in the size of its workforce and consumer base, is beneficial to an economy, boosting demand and economic growth. A shrinking population has the opposite effect.

STABILITY IS JOB ONE

On June 4, 1989, a pro-democracy protest ended in the declaration of Chinese martial law and the death of many civilians in Tiananmen Square. Since then, it has become increasingly clear that strong economic growth, low unemployment, and a rising standard of living are crucial factors supporting social stability and Chinese "harmony," while lessening dissent.

A previous slogan of the Ford Motor Company was "Quality is job one." If China had a slogan, it likely would be "Stability is job one." National support for the Chinese leadership is closely tied to its ability to provide order and deliver jobs. The leadership also understands that since China joined the World Trade Organization in December 2001, much of the country's economic success has been attributable to international trade. In turn, Chinese global engagement also has led to the development of a politically independent and entrepreneurial middle class that, not surprisingly, is demanding more freedoms.

The Chinese government appears to recognize these realities and is under constant pressure to deliver economic opportunity through its brand of one-party capitalism. Some believe that as long as economic advancement is provided in a stable environment, the Chinese population's desire for greater liberties may be muted. But with economic growth projected to be lower in coming years, social stability is becoming an ever larger concern.

As a result, the leadership's laser-like focus on job creation will continue to trump all other domestic and foreign policy concerns in the foreseeable future, a fact that is reflected in the government's level of control and conservative approach to economic issues. It's not surprising that when President George W. Bush reportedly asked former Chinese President Hu Jintao what keeps him up at night, Hu said, "Creating 25 million new jobs a year."

With this goal in mind, the Chinese leadership knows that it must implement new economic reforms. Pressure from ordinary Chinese to advance reforms, and resistance to this from conservative party elites, has presented a difficult challenge for President Xi. Thus, one explanation for the President's high profile anticorruption campaign — which in 2013 alone involved 172,000 corruption cases and 182,000 officials, the Brookings Institution reports — is an attempt to eliminate possible opposition to future reform efforts. These anti-corruption efforts, which continue to consolidate the power of President Xi, also are likely designed to boost credibility for the ruling party.

Moving forward, how well China walks the line between economic reform and political liberties may be as dangerous as a high wire act, as we recently witnessed with student protests in Hong Kong. In an effort to maintain control, China reportedly has reduced tolerance for activism and is closely monitoring non-profit groups, especially those operating in China that are foreign-based.

Once markets are liberalized, history tells us it's only a matter of time before their political systems follow. The adage "open markets open minds" has repeatedly proven true. Look no further than the former Soviet Union to understand what occurs when the flow of information, trade and investment enter authoritarian states. Understanding this trend, China has attempted to walk the line in a distinctly Chinese way and not repeat the mistakes of the former Soviet Union. But walking that line is fraught with risk. In some respects, this highlights dysfunctional aspects of the Chinese system.

The year 2011 marked the point at which the Middle Kingdom's urban population exceeded 50 percent of the country's population, China's National Bureau of Statistics reports. This not only means more than half the country's citizens now live in cities — many of whom recently migrated there from the countryside in search of jobs — but that low-income and somewhat disenfranchised workers exist in larger concentrations. Consequently, if China's economy doesn't perform well, social unrest could spread faster than in the past.

Noted earlier, not long ago Chinese economic growth measured in double digits. In the years ahead, growth is unlikely to exceed 7 percent, the International Monetary Fund reports. Although considered high by developing country standards, this may not be sufficient to generate necessary levels of opportunity that Chinese growth provided in the past.

Although China's leadership may increasingly fear instability, many appear to have developed a seemingly contradictory higher level of confidence for a variety of reasons. For one, due to the global economic crisis that began in the United States, the credibility of the Margaret Thatcher-Ronald Reagan model of free market capitalism has lost some degree of credibility in the eyes of the Chinese. In turn, many in the Middle Kingdom now view their own economic model as superior.

This heightened confidence, combined with China's efforts to develop its own technologies, create national champions, and protect certain industries it considers strategic is reflected in what some American business executives claim is a decreasing level of cooperation foreign firms are receiving from the Chinese government. China's plan to stimulate greater domestic consumption and rely less on the United States and other export markets for future growth is another reason some cite for less cooperation.

Other issues adding tension to the U.S.-China relationship include claims of increasing piracy of American intellectual property, an often arbitrary and inconsistent legal and regulatory environment, a buildup of the Chinese military and its cyber-espionage capabilities, and territorial disputes in the South China and East China Seas, which may be tied to China's need for energy resources.

Plus, China's willingness to subsidize its industries often forces U.S. companies to compete against difficult odds — a problem likely to receive more attention. Chinese subsidies, which are available in many forms, include inexpensive land, artificially low energy costs and taxes, and Chinese bank loans to state-owned companies that go unpaid.

IS CHINA AN INNOVATOR?

A question I'm often asked by audiences and clients is whether or not China is becoming an innovator. The answer is complex.

Demonstrated by innovative clusters like Silicon Valley, which is the envy of the world, the United States continues to be the hub of global innovation. This also is reflected in the fact that 144,621 — approximately half of all utility patents granted by the U.S. Patent and Trademark Office — went to Americans in 2014. America's innovative success is partly the result of the country's acceptance of failure, which is considered part of a normal development process. This attitude also encourages risk taking, an essential ingredient in innovation.

The Japanese proverb, "The nail that pops up is always hammered down," discourages individuals to "go against the grain" or question the process, and instead encourages them to conform to specific norms. As part of Chinese culture, this mindset is seemingly the opposite of the American cultural right to question authority and challenge the system, as in the case of the American Revolutionary War.

"Many people in the West believe that contention and discord lead to breakthroughs, new ideas and innovation. But conflict and disharmony, especially in such serious matters as governance, do not fit the Chinese mentality," says John Naisbitt, the author of *China's Megatrends*. China's cultural reluctance to challenge the status quo does not encourage home-grown innovation.

"The goal of becoming an innovative society cannot be achieved while hierarchical, authoritarian patterns persists in education and in the workplace," Naisbitt remarks. Freedom of inquiry, a Western ideal that has led to independent thinking, is not historically part of the Chinese totalitarian rule. "Modern scientific breakthroughs need people who are willing to question their forefathers' point of view and their bosses' orders," Naisbitt notes. "Hierarchical, authoritarian thinking is China's highest hurdle in changing from the workshop of the world to a leading innovative country."

From a cultural perspective, Chinese business failure also often results in "losing face," which is tantamount to public disgrace. Consequently, it is often repeated that the Chinese would rather do nothing than do something wrong. This mindset also hinders innovation.

My discussion with Chinese students and anecdotal evidence suggests that relative to the population, few students pursue entrepreneurial careers and instead choose positions in state-owned enterprises and government agencies that are considered more secure and connected to the party. In fact, according to Bob Davis, a *Wall Street Journal* senior editor who covers China, "students at Stanford were seven times as likely as those at the most elite Chinese universities to join startups."

But Chinese culture is slowly changing.

The United Nation's World Intellectual Property Organization reports that in 2014, the United States filed 61,492 patent applications under the Patent Cooperation Treaty to hold the top spot. The U.S. was followed by Japan at 42,459. Surprising to many, China advanced to third place, at 25,539, above all European countries.

Tim Ebsary, Director of Business Development for American Commercial Strategies, a California-based firm that works closely with Chinese companies, says "where there is capitalism, there is innovation," and indicates that Chinese innovation is on the rise. Although many Chinese firms are significantly making inroads in innovation, many continue to be dependent on government incentives and the purchasing of new technologies through mergers and acquisitions.

While China currently may not be considered an innovator in the strict sense of the word, its business community certainly knows how to adapt existing technologies and business models, and through an evolving process using many relatively lower paid scientists and technicians, make incremental improvements in products. This process is different than in the United States, where many innovations begin in the garages of millions of entrepreneurs' homes, and considerably different than the typical Chinese process, where the government dominates business, often chooses winners and losers, and invests accordingly.

These economic gambles, if successful, can reward policymakers and workers by creating tremendous numbers of jobs. But if wrong decisions are made, the negative impact, if sustained, can be extremely costly.

FRIENDS CAN ACHIEVE MORE THAN ADVERSARIES

One evening in Nanjing, China, I had dinner in the building that formerly housed the American Embassy. Prior to the end of World War II, Nanjing was the capital of China. This city, which now is the capital of Jiangsu Province, suffered tremendously at the hands of the Japanese in what is known as the Nanjing Massacre. With a common cause, the United States and China became partners in an effort to defeat the Japanese. Today, many in the United States view China as a partner and operate on the basis of friendship. But many do not.

For quite some time, the United States and

China have been mutually dependent: the U.S. has relied on China to finance its debt while China has relied on access to American markets. Although post-recession U.S. imports have slowed and negatively impacted the Chinese economy, the United States and China's bilateral economic relationship continues to run deep.

Most agree that China and the United States should work constructively to overcome difficult obstacles, and that both countries need to better understand what is at stake. The bottom line: How we view China today may determine whether we are friends or adversaries tomorrow. And friends can accomplish a lot more than adversaries.

Since China joined the World Trade Organization in December 2001 to become the 143rd member, U.S. exports to the Middle Kingdom have risen nearly 550 percent, while U.S. exports to the rest of the world have increased 123 percent. This is important because exports of goods and services support millions of American jobs. Prior to joining, China restricted imports through high tariffs and taxes, quotas and other barriers. The Middle Kingdom has come a long way. Currently, China's trade barriers are among the lowest when compared with developing countries.

China's middle class, estimated by the U.S. Department of Commerce to reach 700 million people by

2020, is creating increasing opportunities for American companies, as it demands more and more goods and services from the United States. This trend fits well with China's effort to shift from an export-led model toward a consumer-driven economy.

On the U.S. import side of the equation, China has become the United States' largest foreign supplier of merchandise. This, in effect, subsidizes the standard of living for millions of low and moderate-income American families by keeping the cost of consumer goods down. Noted earlier, imports also benefit American manufacturers with cost-effective materials and components. However, as U.S. trade with China has expanded, imports from China continue to cause concern. But surprising to many, traditional statistics do not capture what is actually occurring.

The bulging U.S. trade deficit with China, at $343 billion in 2014, continues to add tension in our nation's capitol, as well as on factory floors. Although a considerable problem for a variety of reasons, the trade deficit is not accurately measured, and due to sophisticated supply chain management, no longer reflects reality.

About half of Chinese exports to the U.S. are not of Chinese origin, says the U.S. International Trade Commission. Other organizations say it is even less. And if one delves deeply into U.S. high technology imports from China, what is revealed may be surprising.

For example, Apple's 4G iPhone, which not long ago retailed in the United States in excess of $600 if purchased without a wireless phone contract, is assembled in China at a cost of approximately $180. The microchips are made in the United States, the hard drive and display in Japan, and the memory in Korea. China's value-added, which involves labor and no components, is $7.10 per unit or just less than 4 percent of the import cost.[1] Nevertheless, the entire import price, not $7.10, is added to the U.S.-China trade deficit.

Shifting trade patterns also have created new economic realities. Instead of flowing directly to America, today many of Asia's exports first go to China for assembly, processing and manufacturing, and then to the U.S., inflating the U.S.-China trade deficit. In turn, the United States has been purchasing more from China, but less from the rest of Asia. And surprising to many, the proportion of the American trade deficit in 2014 originating in the Pacific Rim, at 57 percent, is actually less than it was in 1998, at 75 percent, according to statistics provided by the Department of Commerce.

U.S. firms interested in doing business in China would be well advised to focus on China's rising middle class, which is increasingly brand conscious.

Consequently, an increasing number of Chinese consumers are willing to pay a premium for high quality American branded goods that validate or reinforce social status.

On the other hand, due to price sensitivities and cultural considerations, many U.S. exporters have found it more effective to develop new products for fast-growing emerging markets, as opposed to modifying higher-end products initially aimed at the United States. Examples of this include General Electric's portable PC-based ultrasound machines developed for rural China, and a handheld electrocardiogram device for rural India — both small and relatively inexpensive, says Jeffrey Immelt, CEO of General Electric. Finally, for U.S. manufacturers who have viewed China solely as a source of low-cost production for American consumers, rising Chinese labor and other costs have cut into their margins.

As a result, a growing number of U.S. producers are moving production to lower cost countries, like Vietnam, Indonesia and Mexico, or back to the United States. But for those companies interested in serving Chinese and other Asian markets, China continues to be a viable manufacturing option.

The size of China's markets differ depending of which metrics are used. For example, based on data from the International Monetary Fund, in 2014 China's GDP was estimated at $10.4 trillion; U.S. GDP was estimated at $17.4 trillion. However, when adjusting for Purchasing Power Parity, which is calculated to reflect the "real cost of living" across countries, China's economy reached at $17.6 trillion — just above the U.S. $17.4 trillion estimate U.S. GDP using Purchasing Power Parity.

Unlike exchange rates, which often are volatile and quick-changing, Purchasing Power Parity attempts to correct for differences in price levels across countries. Simply put, it looks at the number of Chinese renminbi required to buy the same quality haircut in Shanghai as a haircut in New York City.

But there is a downside to using the Purchasing Power Parity methodology. It is more difficult to measure than market-based rates, it requires a tremendous statistical undertaking, and new price comparisons are available only at infrequent intervals that could reduce accuracy. Additionally, not everyone agrees on the methodology. As a result, economic estimates from various organizations and scholars differ.

For example, Arvind Subramanian, senior fellow at the Peterson Institute for International Economics and the Center for Global Development, and senior research professor at Johns Hopkins University, said based on Purchasing Power Parity, China's output surpassed U.S.

output years ago. He anticipates the Chinese economy will be twice as large as the United States' by 2030.

From an individual perspective, using Purchasing Power Parity metrics also boosts Chinese per capita income. "The different approaches to valuing economic output and resources are not just of theoretical interest," says Subramanian. "They have real world significance, especially in the balance of power and economic dominance."

Purchasing power parity, which in the case of China significantly shows higher output, may actually provide a more realistic picture of various Chinese economic strengths and abilities. For example, using Purchasing Power Parity, China's tremendous and fast-expanding shipbuilding industry output may be better understood, illuminating the fact that the Middle Kingdom has recently built many of the world's largest ports capable of handling tremendous amounts of trade measured by both cargo volume and container traffic. Additionally, this methodology may better explain how China has come to be world's largest manufacturer. The bottom line: traditional statistics may have undervalued Chinese capabilities and underestimated its output, along with other developing countries.

When viewing various countries using Purchasing Power Parity, the world's economic landscape changes considerably. For example, India, Brazil, Indonesia and Mexico move up compared with other countries. When considering per capita income, the new methodology increases the income in developing countries compared with developed ones, indicating that the income gap between the two groups has decreased.

STRATEGIES THAT WORK

International engagement is an increasingly important generator of American economic and corporate growth. Millions of higher-paying, higher-skilled jobs are dependent on it. But to succeed, it's essential that government policies are implemented that create an environment in which companies can thrive. American companies, small and large, must understand the forces operating in the global environment that can help or hinder their efforts.

HIDDEN RISKS AND INTERNATIONAL STRATEGIES

When engaging internationally through exporting, importing, investing abroad or establishing strategic alliances with foreign partners, it's critical to understand the hidden risks. If not, using an unethical supplier can result in endless lawsuits, while poor market opportunities can generate tremendous losses. On the other hand, correctly grasping foreign market wants, needs and abilities can lead to great success. To make your job easier, consider the following strategies that have been conveniently summarized. Note that several of these have been discussed in a broader context in previous chapters.

Investigate Intellectual Property Protection

Many countries claim to enforce intellectual property laws, but have poor track records. If your products are intellectually rich, investigate how piracy is handled in a given country. If intellectual property protection isn't a priority or very effective, it may be wise to steer clear of these markets.

Intellectual property and innovation play a central role in driving productivity and overall growth in the U.S. economy. In fact, the U.S. International Trade Commission says intellectual property and technological innovation have been associated with approximately three-quarters of the United States' average annual economic growth since the mid-1940s.

As such, much of today's intellectual property is incorporated into products and services that make them considerably more attractive internationally. This is attributable to efforts often associated with great expense. Additionally, improvements in a manufacturing process, know-how or practical knowledge that deliver greater efficiencies also can carry a large price tag. As a result, it's important that intellectual property be employed as effectively as possible and protected from piracy.

According to the World Intellectual Property Organization, a United Nations agency, "intellectual property shall include the rights relating to:

- Literary, artistic and scientific works,
- Performances of performing artists, phonograms, and broadcasts,
- Inventions in all fields of human endeavor,
- Scientific discoveries,
- Industrial designs,
- Trademarks, service marks, and commercial names and designations,
- Protection against unfair competition, and
- All other rights resulting from intellectual activity in the industrial, scientific, literary or artistic fields."

As stated by Vincent LoTempio, an Intellectual Property (IP) lawyer and author located in Upstate New York, three types of IP are commonly protected through registrations. These are:

1. Copyrights, which include literary and artistic works, such as movies, novels, poems, plays,

music, paintings, software, and architectural designs,

2. Trademarks, which include brands, logos and company names, and

3. Patents, which can cover new, useful and non-obvious improvements of machines, articles of manufacture, methods of doing business, and compositions of matter.

Other forms of intellectual property that can be protected by lawsuit if copied without permission or surreptitiously obtained include industrial designs, trade secrets (ex. Coca Cola's formula), and geographical indications of source (ex. Burgundy Wine), LoTempio says.

Theft of intellectual property continues to be a major problem and the costs are staggering. The bottom line: stronger copyright law enforcement by governments and international organizations is extremely important to preserve the integrity of the global trading system. Companies should also implement various strategies to protect their intellectual property.

Registering patents, trademarks and other intellectual property with appropriate agencies in countries where companies sell or produce products is an important early step in protecting a company's

intellectual property, says LoTempio. But first, companies are wise to establish a strategy to properly identify their intellectual property. LoTempio says this could be as simple as:

- Educating employees so they understand and can document what is patentable subject matter,
- Creating a patent review committee to evaluate potential inventions,
- Establishing a decision-making process to assess the anticipated cost and financial benefits of filing for a patent, and
- Assigning action steps to qualified individuals to implement the strategy.

The burden of demonstrating intellectual property theft can be a costly endeavor. And companies that bring formal charges in countries where IP infringements occur sometimes fear retaliation or being locked out of lucrative markets. Nevertheless, the cost of doing nothing often far exceeds the cost of protecting intellectual property. And very importantly, since intellectual property represents much of today's competitive advantage, protecting or not protecting your IP could mean the difference between success and failure.

Design Products for Specific Markets

In the past, U.S. manufacturers typically produced products for the domestic market, then later adapted them for developing country market needs. That's changed. Due to their increasingly greater market size, more and more U.S. firms are specifically designing products for emerging markets that are not likely to sell in the United States.

For example, General Electric designed a portable PC-based ultrasound machine for rural China, and a handheld electrocardiogram device for rural India — both small and relatively inexpensive, said Jeffrey Immelt, CEO of General Electric. International sales of these products, which were not offered in the United States, reportedly were very favorable.

Closely Monitor Suppliers

Due to the ever-changing nature of international business, corporate global supply chains are becoming increasingly sophisticated. In turn, companies are optimizing their supply chains by controlling costs, updating infrastructure, implementing green practices, and offering more intense employee training. Unfortunately, too many are not closely monitoring who is supplying their products.

When U.S. firms delve deeply into their supply

chains, it's sometimes revealed that with successive production runs, low-cost country manufacturers have shifted to lower quality suppliers or simply cut corners to drive costs down without the knowledge of the contractor or buyer. A widely-reported example of this includes Mattel, a U.S. toy manufacturer that had to recall millions of foreign-made toys made in China because they were contaminated with lead paint.

Protect Against Currency and Political Risks

Importers from countries with soft currencies or insufficient reserves may find it difficult to pay for products delivered. Consequently, it's essential to understand the risks and work closely with your banker to minimize them. Should your firm accept the importer's currency, guard against wide fluctuations.

Keep abreast of political risks. Should a military coup take place, a succeeding government may reverse policy. And if social turmoil envelops a nation, the disruption of activities could put your company out of business. Keep in mind that new governments have been known to reverse policy with regard to a wide range of investment and trade issues.

Understand the Legal System

In some countries, the accused is presumed guilty until

proven innocent, and judges may unfairly favor domestic sales agents terminated over poor performance or consumers who are injured by the inappropriate use of a product. One of the most pressing issues in doing business abroad is the lack of civil, commercial and criminal codes. Additionally, confusing and burdensome bureaucratic requirements can tie up valuable time. That's why one must carefully assess each target country's laws and practices, and determine if you wish to expose your company to them.

Also, keep in mind that environmental standards greatly differ from country to country. Certain machinery may not meet stringent foreign environmental pollution standards, which could prevent product importation. On the other hand, some developing countries may not provide adequate facilities to treat or store toxic byproducts generated by a manufacturing process, which could create serious health risks and legal problems.

Accurately Assess the Barriers To Trade

Identify each selected market's trade barriers — tariffs, as well as standards, regulations, quotas, labeling requirements, etc. If excessive, these barriers may make your products too expensive and limit their exports. If manageable, investigate whether any vested interests can bar your product from the market.

It's also important to know your competitors' products, prices, distribution methods, commitments to after-sale service, and target customers. If intense competition exists, it may be wise to consider smaller markets which may be unattractive for multinationals, but big enough for your firm.

Be Familiar with Purchasing Trends

To determine how much of your product is imported by target markets, here's what to do. First, rank each potential country market by the dollar value of your product imported from the United States. Then rank each market by its total demand (domestic production plus world imports) for the previous three years. This will determine each country's market size, its rate of growth, U.S. market share, and whether product demand is increasing or decreasing.

If total demand for your type of product is increasing, look at the country's rate of growth and per capita income. If indicators are positive, it's likely that your product demand will continue to rise. However, if these indicators are stagnant or down, it's likely that the growth in demand for your product will slow and may not provide the market potential hoped for.

Consider Infrastructure Needs

If a firm's product requires a skilled support staff (human infrastructure), it's essential to make sure such staffing is available in your target markets. If not, a U.S. exporter may be forced to provide costly support from its home office.

The lack of physical infrastructure also can curtail exports. For example, the inability to quickly deliver perishables due to inoperable roads or inaccessibility to refrigerated storage can be a deterrent. The shipping costs of heavy merchandise to distant locations also may prove too expensive. In this case, a firm may wish to consider licensing its technology instead of exporting the product.

Emphasize the American Brand

As products become commoditized, customers worldwide appear to be increasingly brand conscious. In fact, many consumers in developing countries are motivated to pay relatively large sums for American branded products that reinforce their social status. This not only helps to sell American-made products abroad, it enhances long-term customer loyalty.

Today, there are approximately 1.8 billion middle class consumers. By 2030, the OECD estimates this figure will rise to 5 billion with the vast majority living in Asia.

HOW TO BOOST EFFICIENCIES AND PREVENT SUPPLY CHAIN DISASTERS

Whoever said "if it ain't broke, don't fix it" probably lived in a simpler time. Today, one must be proactive, not reactive, and anticipate problems before they occur. As in many industries, simple problems can easily turn into big ones if preventative measures aren't implemented. And the supply chain business, more so than many others, is no exception.

Building, managing and sustaining efficient global supply chains are necessary for an increasing number of companies. But this activity is fraught with risks and challenges, and can be very expensive. To reduce risks, issues regularly affecting a supply chain must be addressed in innovative ways. Companies can optimize their global supply chains by properly controlling costs, updating infrastructure, pursuing cross-functional alignment, implementing green practices, and offering more effective employee training.

Supply chain functions should not be viewed as independent and separate activities, disconnected from other corporate departments. They must work seamlessly together with other company functions if spending is to be balanced. If not, meeting the objectives of one department, like manufacturing, may result in excessive costs in other areas, like logistics.

For example, if a California-based company receives supplies from several Asian firms, and in turn, incorporates those inputs in production that is shipped to Canadian customers, expenses related to Asian manufacturing may appear very beneficial. But when factoring in costs associated with the supply chain, which include transportation, warehousing, security, and quality control, the entire operation may be at a loss. And this could be the case even if the Asian costs are only a small slice of overall expenses.

The expense of maintaining a healthy supply chain is frequently overwhelming. According to a 2013 Survey by PricewaterhouseCoopers, an international business consulting firm, 80 percent of those who work in supply chain management consider reducing their total supply chain cost to be a top priority. Use of a thorough performance metrics system can help a company discover weaknesses in its system. It can identify which business practices and employee functions bring the least or most value to an operation. And by understanding what is specifically required to achieve a successful just-in-time inventory, a company can avoid unnecessary costs related to overstocking.

A wider knowledge of the global economic situation and a tightening of a supply chain's managerial core also are of vital importance. By identifying countries or regions with low-cost suppliers and keeping managerial staff limited, analysts say a company can substantially lower supply chain expenses.

Keeping infrastructure up-to-date and well maintained is key to a successful supply chain. But many companies and countries have failed to adjust to the infrastructure demands of the 21st century. This is not only a major problem overseas, but for the United States as well.

The American transportation infrastructure, including ports, roads, rail and airports, is aging and requires critical attention. In fact, according to a bipartisan panel of experts and two former secretaries of transportation, Norman Mineta and Samuel Skinner, an additional $134 billion to $262 billion must be spent per year through 2035 to rebuild roads, bridges, rail systems, and air transportation. And that estimate does not include the costs to maintain and upgrade the nation's ports.

According to former Secretary of Commerce Gary Locke, "We are placing rapidly growing demands on aging infrastructure systems. We need to find new methods to move products more efficiently if we are to keep pace with the rest of the world." Not only does inadequate investment in infrastructure increase a company's expenses and raise the price of items on store shelves, there is a human cost as well, as failing infrastructure takes lives and causes injuries.

By updating America's transportation infrastructure, costs of transporting goods to and from American factories and warehouses can be reduced. On the other hand, individual companies also can bend the cost curve on long term operating expenses involving warehousing, inventory, and their transportation infrastructure. The impact can be enormous. A study by Boston Strategies International found that reducing freight transportation costs by ten percent resulted in a one percent decrease in overall operating expenses.

"We are at a pivotal moment when it comes to maintaining and modernizing our nation's infrastructure. Many of our roads, bridges, water systems, and our national electric grid were put into place over fifty years ago, and these systems are simply overwhelmed or worn out," says Gregory E. DiLoreto, President of The American Society of Civil Engineers. The 2013 Report Card for America's Infrastructure gives an overall grade of D+ across 16 categories, up just slightly from the D given in the organization's 2009 report card. This slight improvement is due to upgrades and repairs resulting from an increase in private, state and federal targeted investments.

The movement of goods across the United States, which will continue to accelerate due to a projected increase in imports and exports, will put greater stress on an already fatigued system of American roads, highways and bridges. In fact, according to the report *Freight Facts and Figures 2013* published by the U.S. Department of Transportation, the U.S. movement of tonnage due to international trade is projected to grow at an annual rate of 3.4 percent between 2007 and 2040.

"Over two hundred million trips are taken daily across deficient bridges in the nation's 102 largest metropolitan regions. In total, one in nine of the nation's bridges are rated as structurally deficient, while the average age of the nation's 607,380 bridges is currently 42 years," The American Society of Civil Engineers reports.

"Transportation systems are the backbone of America. They keep our nation strong and moving. But we have not been taking good care of this resource. Lacking a coherent vision for our transportation future and chronically short of resources, we defer new investments, fail to plan and allow existing systems to fall into disrepair," says the Miller Center of Public Affairs at the University of Virginia.

In 1966, President Lyndon B. Johnson stated

that, "Modern transportation can be the rapid conduit of economic growth — or a bottleneck." In recent years, it appears to have become a bottleneck.

A failure to improve America's infrastructure, especially its ports, will have a tremendous negative impact. According to a 2012 report by The American Society of Civil Engineers, "If America only maintains its current level of investment in these systems, the losses to its economy will increase shipping costs annually. By 2020, lost value of exports will be $270 billion and will rise to almost $2 trillion by 2040. The cumulative loss in national GDP will be about $700 billion by 2020 and reach $4 trillion by 2040." And looking forward, many American ports will not be prepared to handle the much larger ships that will pass through the expanded Panama Canal.

The Panama Canal expansion project, which was initially scheduled to be completed in 2014, 100 years after its first opening, has been delayed for a number of reasons. Nevertheless, on December 31, 2014, the Panama Canal Authority said its new locks are expected to be tested at the end of 2015 and be ready for commercial transit in early 2016.

In 1881, France began working on the canal but discontinued efforts after encountering engineering problems and staggering death rates due to disease.

The United States, which took over the project in 1904, completed the canal in 1914. A century later, the expansion of the canal will accommodate Post-Panamax vessels: ships 235 feet longer and 54 feet wider than the Panama vessels that can handle up to 12,600 TEUs — twenty-foot equivalent unit shipping containers 20' x 8' x 8.5'. By undertaking its current expansion, Panama will double its canal's capacity.

To handle Post-Panamax vessels, dredging and upgrading berthing areas to 50-foot depths is required in most American ports, as well as replacing gantry cranes with cranes having the height and reach to unload taller and wider container vessels, says Colliers International, a leader in commercial real estate. Other infrastructure improvements, including the raising of surrounding bridges, need to be made in some cases.

It is estimated that more than 70 percent of U.S. container traffic from Asia passes through Pacific ports, and as much as a third of those containers travel through Los Angeles and Long Beach. But once the expansion project is completed, container ships traversing through the Panama Canal from Asia will be able to make port calls at American ports in the South and East Coast. However, only a few of these ports are Post-Panamax ready; others are racing to catch up.

While port authorities and their private sector

partners planned over $46 billion in capital improvements from 2013 through 2016, The American Society of Civil Engineers says federal funding has declined for navigable waterways and landside freight connections needed to move goods to and from the ports. As a result of this and other factors, The American Society of Civil Engineers' last report card, published in 2013, gave American ports a grade of C.

The Miller Center says, "Our chief trading partners are making significant investments in their transportation infrastructure; America must do the same to remain competitive." To compete with emerging economic powerhouses like China, the United States needs to become more efficient. And this includes making investments in all transportation infrastructure. Not surprisingly, of the world's largest container ports measured in TEUs in 2013, Los Angeles and Long Beach ranked among the world's 19th and 21st largest ports. The Port of New York/New Jersey ranked 27th. Ten Chinese ports ranked in the top 18.

Investing in information technology also is essential for supply chain infrastructure development. Enterprise Resource Planning (ERP) technology is widely used to better organize and unify supply chain processes. Companies also are increasingly embracing the benefits of "cloud computing" or Internet sharing of software and information resources as they take advantage of useful new technological capabilities.

Technology can further be applied to support cross-functional alignment. Cloud computing, ERP implementation, and use of performance metrics all assist in integrating the activities of various corporate departments. Cross-functional integration, however, requires more than information sharing and performance evaluating. Employees should also have a clear understanding of their roles within the supply chain network.

Once structural and technological processes that encourage integration are in place, analysts say the focus should then be placed on establishing concrete interdepartmental connections. Collaboration between those working in separate departments of a company is aided by awareness of an organization's larger mission. Flow charts and other materials may express how a company's different sectors intersect and rely upon one another.

As cross-functional alignment becomes a reality, a fluid, better united company generally emerges. Supply chain management is more proficiently executed when thoughtful interdepartmental cooperation occurs.

While improving a supply chain's performance, "green" factors should also be considered. Developing a green supply chain can generate more business as companies are applauded for reducing their carbon footprint. Many environmentally conscious actions also have the benefit of lowering supply chain costs.

A company can create a more eco-friendly supply chain and save money in the long run by:

1. Switching from paper to electronic processes,
2. Ensuring transportation routes used are the shortest and most direct possible,
3. Outsourcing to data centers instead of maintaining on-site centers,
4. Reducing the amount of energy utilized, and
5. Cultivating relationships with green suppliers.

Surprising to many, small changes to supply chain operations can have a tremendous impact on the environment. Maintaining a greener supply chain is a cost-effective way to show a company is vested not only in its future, but also in the future of the world.

Perhaps of most importance to a successful supply chain are the employees who make the chain run smoothly. Without well informed and motivated workers, a supply chain cannot function efficiently and effectively, resulting in delivery delays and monetary losses. Based on the PricewaterhouseCoopers survey, almost three-fifths of supply chain management executives say there is a deficit in much needed talent.

In order to compensate for the lack of talent, many companies have chosen to offer more intensive training. Supply chain management academies have risen to meet a demand for comprehensive worker education, greatly increasing the knowledge base and expertise of those responsible for complex supply networks. Frequently, trainee education is financed by the employer to encourage superior work.

Although sound supply chain management practices are not always followed, pursuing a careful supply chain strategy is important. And the benefits are large. A well-oiled supply chain can go a long way in enhancing global competitiveness and achieving higher profits. It also could be the difference between success and failure.

As businesses successfully address cost concerns, infrastructure needs, cross-functional integration, greening, and employee education, companies can strengthen their organizations as a whole. Supply chains are the veins through which international trade flows. But what happens to companies when seemingly reliable supply chains are disrupted or break down?

It is virtually impossible to accurately assess and understand the impact of the untold risks a supply chain may incur. And there are many reasons for this, including the presence of "black swans."

A black swan devastated Japan in March 2011 through a series of highly unlikely events, including an earthquake that produced a tsunami, and ultimately, a nuclear crisis. As a result, Japanese suppliers were paralyzed for months. This resulted in the breakdown of global and U.S. supply chains.

For those managing a company's supply chain, deliveries may be severely delayed or no longer available in the wake of wars, terrorist threats, civil strife, strikes, natural disasters, severe storms, or other factors. Due to the inability or unlikelihood of predicting various risks, companies participating in worldwide supply networks must carefully consider how they will react if the flow of supplies is negatively impacted for whatever reasons.

Thus, an American company relying on supplies from a Canadian factory must anticipate delays due to border security issues. But it also must contemplate delays caused by a variety of unknown factors and plan accordingly. The bottom line: companies need to be concerned about the stability of their supply chains. Disruptions to supply chains due to environmental problems such as natural disasters and extreme weather were cited as the least manageable.

Companies can address such uncontrollable

risks by maintaining relationships with backup supply providers in different parts of the world. According to Nick Wildgoose, a supply chain expert at Zurich Financial Services, companies may be forced to look beyond "tier one suppliers" for the sake of a stable supply chain.

Although a supplier may appear attractive because of certain factors, such as low manufacturing and assembly costs or high product quality, location issues could trump these and other considerations. An ideal supplier, whether used for primary or for contingency purposes, must be selected after careful consideration of various factors, including environmental, geopolitical, and economic conditions in the supplier's home country or region.

A supply chain also may be strengthened or protected through the presence of backup inventories. Although this necessitates additional costs, the vital time afforded by stockpiled resources may provide enough time to remedy a problem. Given the precariousness of global trade stability, as seen through the chaos and infrastructure breakdown caused by natural disasters, a well-stocked inventory could be a savior for a supply chain in need of rescue.

Furthermore, Steve Culp of Accenture Risk Management advises that companies keep detailed track of their supply chain logistics, monitoring and quantifying risk through a clear performance metrics system. By compiling and tracking statistics on fill rates, delivery delays, and other pertinent factors affecting a supply chain, a company can identify weaknesses and inconsistencies in a network. If risk can be better analyzed, it can be better addressed.

Known and unknown risks will always be present in supply chain systems. Sound supply chain management requires an awareness of potential risks, a well-chosen selection of primary and alternative suppliers, and, if possible, a just-in-case inventory of vital supplies if just-in-time deliveries fail.

FINANCING GLOBAL
SUPPLY CHAIN ACTIVITIES

The financing of global supply chains, which involves all transactions relating to cash flow from the buyer's purchase order through payment to the seller, is just as essential as maintaining an efficient supply chain. Due to the ever-changing nature of international business, supply chains and the ability to finance their activities, are becoming increasingly sophisticated. For example, an importer in Ohio may contract with suppliers in South Korea, Taiwan and Japan to produce components, which are then shipped to China for assembly, and when completed, shipped to the Ohio importer. This activity may be continuous, necessitating multiple purchase orders, and delivery and payment schedules.

Although many U.S. importers and exporters manage less complicated supply chains, the financial issues faced and end goals are very similar. For example, exporters and importers generally wish to:

1. Streamline operations and reduce costs,
2. Better integrate and align often-fragmented financial supply chains with physical supply chains,
3. Improve efficiencies, which often includes switching from a paper-based accounting process to an electronic one,
4. Develop more stable and secure supply chains, and
5. Improve buyer-seller relationships.

On the other hand, some interests are very different: importers typically wish to extend payment terms as long as possible, while exporters desire quick payments, improved terms, and reduced "days sales outstanding" (DSO), thereby lowering working capital requirements. How can these interests be reconciled? By discounting a time draft under a bank guarantee or letter of credit (a very simple solution), both exporters and importers can be highly satisfied. And the costs to achieve this are relatively low.

For decades, traditional supply chain financing has involved manually managing letters of credit and documentary collection activities. Increasingly, however, these functions are being woven into state-of-the-art software systems that automate the entire financial supply chain process. By utilizing this type of platform, financial supply chain efficiencies can be optimized. And both exporters and importers can obtain their objectives while improving their level of competitiveness. The benefits are significant and often include:

1. A reduction of working capital needs and improved cash flow due to reduced DSO,

2. Lower financing rates due to decreased levels of risk,

3. The ability to improve inventory control and minimize costs by utilizing just-in-time techniques due to more accurate forecasting and greater predictability of financial flows, and

4. Greater insight into supply chain activities and possible problems through timely and continuous information availability.

Additionally, from the perspective of the importer, if the financial supply chain solution reduces the need to issue letters of credit, then valuable lines of credit which have become tied up can now be available for other purposes. But the benefits don't stop there.

Whether it is vendor financing, letters of credit or receivables financing, effectively managing financial supply chain operations can eliminate what many view as a complicated and burdensome endeavor. The entire process can be made easier by working with knowledgeable professionals and utilizing automated systems capable of aligning supply chain finance needs with the goals and objectives of both importers and exporters.

A financial institution's ability to better connect its people and systems to those of its clients can help companies achieve long term goals. And through this strategy, financial institutions, exporters and importers are better able to streamline the financial supply chain process, and in turn, improve efficiencies and speed achievement of objectives.

Managing the hazards related to international deals is more crucial today than ever. And the risks extend well beyond those precipitated by the recent financial crisis — from payment defaults, foreign exchange fluctuations and political instability, to piracy and risks posed by natural disasters. Successfully managing a global supply chain is not easy. But optimizing your financial supply chain does not have to be difficult.

THE IMPORTANCE OF UNDERSTANDING CULTURE

If you're doing business abroad, understanding the host country culture is paramount. Culture is defined as a collection of values, beliefs, behaviors, customs, and attitudes that distinguish a society. It is learned and interrelated, defines group membership and differences, and can't be ignored.

Today, cultural perspectives are at work in just about every endeavor, including hiring, firing, compensation, etiquette, negotiating, office setting, and strategy. But culture also plays a major role in understanding why certain behaviors, including terrorism, exist to the extent that they do. In short, if a foreign culture is not respected, the relationship is likely to suffer.

Attitudes and societal values differ considerably throughout the world. In fact, acceptable behavior in one cultural setting may be viewed as immoral, unethical or rude in another. For example, "kickbacks," while expected in some developing countries may land you in jail in others. And nepotism, while prevalent in some areas of the world, is frowned upon in others, since it may result in incompetence and inefficiencies.

Many cultures have specific customs worth noting. In India, for instance, since the left hand is considered unclean, the right hand should be used for eating, giving and accepting. In Malaysia, pointing with the index finger is considered impolite; it is more appropriate to point with the thumb of the right hand with the fingers folded under. Furthermore, in France, a firm and pumping handshake is considered uncultured, while in the Middle East, you should not point your finger at someone or show the soles of your feet when seated. The soles are considered unclean and offensive.

Many cultures also view time and status very differently. For example, Germans tend to be very punctual, paying much attention to the small hands on a clock. To the contrary, Latin Americans and Italians tend to have a more relaxed sense of time. This means that a German business person may arrive at 3:50 for a 4:00 appointment, while a Latin American business person may arrive at 4:15. Without understanding cultural differences surrounding punctuality, the value of a meeting may come into question.

Work standards or ethics also are relative. Generally, U.S. and German business people are considered driven and deterministic. This can lead to poor results during meetings with those from different cultures. When abroad, U.S. business people generally prefer to get right down to business. To others, this is considered premature and does not help establish a friendship — a prerequisite to doing business in many countries. In Saudi Arabia, for example, the initial business meeting is designed to establish a relationship and build mutual trust. As such, business usually is not even discussed.

For those doing business in Japan, it is imperative to know that Japanese culture is defined in hierarchical terms with the good of the group reigning supreme. In this case, emphasis is placed on seniority and group well-being instead of individual performance and needs. As a result, seeking a decision from an individual without a group consensus is extremely difficult. Similarly, status, which can be identified by titles on business cards, signifies much importance throughout Asia. When deciding who to address or determining the level of formality to use while speaking to an individual, be sure to consider his or her status.

In addition to expressed customs, nonverbal communication is also very important because the meaning behind gestures and facial expressions can vary significantly. For example, nodding "yes" in the United States is equivalent to "no" in Bulgaria. Overall, body posture, positioning, and eye contact may influence how one is perceived. Take for instance the following example: the joining of the thumb and forefinger in a circle while extending the other three fingers means "OK" in the United States. However, in Malta, this symbol signifies homosexuality; in Japan, money; in France, inadequacy; and in many parts of Eastern Europe, vulgarity.

In many cultures, employees sometimes will say "yes" to their ability to complete a task even though they have no intention of doing so. Why? In the employees' eyes, saying no to a manager may be considered disrespectful or rude. Or, the employee may feel compelled to say "yes" for fear of losing face. Thus, the employee would rather lie than seem incapable of performance. Understanding the motive behind the "yes" may help improve a poor working relationship.

One typical obstacle to building a successful international relationship is ethnocentric behavior. This form of arrogance reflects little desire to accept or adapt to the host country's culture, including communicating in the host's country's language. When U.S. firms establish foreign subsidiaries, some tend to implement a policy of "one size fits all," and don't consider different cultural modes of doing business. This ethnocentric behavior is often regarded by host country employees, managers, and suppliers as rude, and is perceived as an unwillingness to respect the host country's culture and standards.

To counter this behavior, it is extremely wise for U.S. business people to speak the host country's language whenever possible. Even simply attempting to communicate in the host country's native tongue can work wonders in demonstrating mutual respect and a willingness to work together.

U.S. corporations operating in foreign countries often act as agents of change, bringing new operating standards, state-of-the-art technology, values, and best business practices, which in turn, may contribute to the improvement of the host country's social, labor, and environmental conditions. This, no doubt, can and has generated very positive relations for U.S. firms, and has gone a long way toward building positive and long-lasting relationships. However, not being culturally sensitive can certainly result in missed opportunities.

AMERICA'S SECRET SAUCE

In October 1957 when the former Soviet Union launched Sputnik, the first artificial satellite, the United States became acutely aware of its technological abilities and shortcomings. Since the 1960s, when American ingenuity put men on the moon and safely returned them home, the United States has continued to dominate the world in terms of investment in research and development. According to the latest data from the National Science Foundation, even on a Purchasing Power Parity basis the United States still spends more than twice as much as China, the next largest research and development spender.

American research and development funding, along with the tremendous technological breakthroughs advanced by U.S. companies, universities and the military, have had an extremely beneficial impact on virtually every sector and every American.

Due to the amazing progress in technology and significant reductions in its cost (noted earlier, the now-dated iPhone 4 offers roughly the same performance as a $5 million 1975 supercomputer), America's modern-life conveniences — from laptop computers, big screen televisions, and smart phones, to air conditioners, washers, dryers, refrigerators, and advanced medical technologies — have provided the vast majority of Americans with conveniences that in the past were only accessible by relatively wealthy consumers. Consequently, when considering our standard of living, it's important to look beyond household median income.

For example, take our much criticized health care system. Despite the fact that the United States spends considerably more per person than other countries on health care and fails to achieve better health outcomes than other countries, I have the highest regard for American hospitals, U.S.-trained physicians and advanced U.S. medical technology.

In the spring of 2015, I had the displeasure of witnessing extremely poor health care being administered to my son Christopher, who was critically injured while vacationing in Latin America. Upon my and his mother's arrival at the Latin American public hospital, we found the conditions horrific. The floors and walls were filthy, the staff did not wear gloves, and the hospital bathrooms did not have soap, toilet seats, toilet paper or towels. We even were told to purchase medical supplies at a local store.

At the hospital, I hired a private nurse to keep a close eye on my son. I also began to search for better care for Chris, as over the course of just two days his health deteriorated. I attempted to obtain his discharge from the public hospital and move him to a private hospital to be treated by a U.S.-trained doctor. However, due to the incredible inefficiency of the staff, it took over five hours to pay the hospital bill and obtain the discharge documents. At this point, I was no longer able to contact the doctor at the private hospital to have Christopher transferred there.

Ultimately, not knowing if the private hospital had the necessary technology and medical requirements, and with the advice of medical professionals in the United States, Christopher's mother and I decided to depart that evening for the United States to obtain better health care for our son. Once our plane landed, Christopher was immediately taken to one of America's finest trauma centers. There, he was evaluated and rushed into a second emergency surgery.

The U.S. doctor later informed me that the Latin American doctor botched the first surgery. I also was told that if Christopher had not received the second surgery, he would have died within 24 to 48 hours. The advanced health care received by my son is another example of the American standard of living I will not soon forget.

In addition to advanced U.S. health care, our American system also has produced companies like Facebook, Apple, Google and Microsoft — organizations that would have emerged and prospered in few other countries. But it's not just America's technology and culture of innovation at work here.

THE INGREDIENTS

America's "secret sauce" has provided tremendous advantages. The "secret sauce" includes the U.S. system of free market capitalism, capital markets, rule of law, separation of church and state, entrepreneurialism, balance of power, the welcoming of immigrants, and a brilliant Constitution. Combined, these factors have promoted stability and created an environment empowering people to unleash their creativity to achieve their dreams.

The role of immigrants and the wisdom of the framers of the Constitution cannot be emphasized enough. In many cases, the immigrants were young people like my grandparents who left their homelands with little hope of ever seeing their parents again, but with tremendous hope of securing a better future. They understood the difficulties they would incur, but possessed the necessary courage and resolve to persevere. This strength and determination continues to be reflected in all that is American.

To borrow a phrase from Lord John Acton, a member of British Parliament in the 1860s, the framers of the U.S. Constitution understood an important fact: "absolute power corrupts absolutely." The American experiment, which was founded on a philosophy and not a bloodline, clearly sets the U.S. apart. These factors, which promote opportunity regardless of individual differences, in great part are why America is the most powerful nation on Earth.

Although not flawless, capitalism has generated the greatest economic growth the world has ever seen. At the core of its brilliance is its ability to create incentives to produce solutions to problems, and to distribute those solutions broadly. And in doing so, it has paved the way for tremendous gains in efficiency and productivity.

When discussing its benefits, Michael Novak said "No other system so rapidly raises up the living standards of the poor, so thoroughly improves the conditions of life, or generates greater social wealth and distributes it more broadly. In the long competition of the last 100 years, neither socialist nor third-world experiments have performed as well in improving the lot of common people, paid higher wages, and more broadly multiplied liberties and opportunities."

Novak indicated that a free society requires economic liberty. As noted earlier, he also stressed that checks and balances are to the political order what competition is to capitalism. Unlike many other countries, America is fortunate to have a strong system of checks and balances, as well as one that promotes competition. Nevertheless, Novak stresses the need to ensure these systems are well maintained.

Few nations possess the American-like system of checks and balances that prevents any one group from permanently imposing its will on others. This balance is part of an important American formula that shepherds constant changes — some good, some bad — but always allowing for self correction. With all its flaws, for generations countless numbers of people worldwide have wanted to participate in the American experience.

After dozens of speaking engagements in Mexico in the early 1990s, I found that many in the audience either had an American passport or badly wanted one. When I crossed through *Check Point Charlie* from West Berlin to East Berlin in March 1990, it was like entering a time warp. The grey unkempt landscape and dilapidated buildings in the former German Democratic Republic, known as Communist East Germany, looked as though that country hadn't been repaired since combat-ready American and Soviet tanks faced off yards apart in one of the world's most tense nuclear showdowns. While there I witnessed the dismantling of the Berlin Wall and observed the first free parliamentary elections held in that region since 1933. I also was told by countless East Germans of their wish to move to the United States in order to seek a better life.

When visiting Nanjiang, China, I had the opportunity to address the Jiangsu Academy of Social Sciences, the provincial government think tank. Not surprisingly, I was asked about various problems associated with the United States' political system. I could not help recalling a quote by Winston Churchill, who when asked about problems with democracy said, "It's the worse system except for all the others." I answered the question and then explained how I believed China's leadership has made some excellent economic decisions for its country, especially with regard to how it spent its stimulus funds designed to ensure its economy would not falter after the Great Recession. But then I asked in a more polite way than this: what if future generations of Chinese leaders are not as intelligent?

On a post-Great Recession trip to China, I sensed a heightened patriotism and a new confidence in the Chinese system, often referred to as "socialism with Chinese characteristics." Still, young Chinese I meet often tell me of their desire to study in or permanently move to the United States. I have found this desire is shared by students from all over the world.

Some economic systems, no doubt, are better than others. Although the fall of the Berlin Wall marked the end of communism in the former Soviet Union, that system began collapsing under its own weight many years prior to this historic event. As the saying went: people pretended to work and the government pretended to pay them. It's no surprise that the level of productivity and accountability was abysmal. With few incentives to produce, output was poor; quality was worse.

As the communist system was disintegrating, I met with several corporate chief executives in then Soviet-dominated Poland. Interestingly, not one could tell me what it cost to manufacture their goods. What they did tell me was startling: when supplies were delivered, people worked; when supplies ran out, the workers went home. It's no surprise why that system performed miserably.

Many people, including Mikhail Gorbachev, the last General Secretary of the former Soviet Union, Pope John Paul II, and U.S. President Ronald Reagan played very important roles in accelerating communism's demise. From the time he took office in 1981, Reagan increased financial and military pressure on the Soviet Union.

On June 12, 1987, his famous speech, which was heard around the world, reflected his position throughout his presidency. President Reagan stood at the Brandenburg Gate in former West Berlin and said, "General Secretary Gorbachev, if you seek peace, if you seek prosperity for the Soviet Union and Eastern Europe, if you seek liberation: Come here to this gate! Mr. Gorbachev, open this gate! Mr. Gorbachev, tear down this wall!"

Two years later, on November 9, 1989, the Berlin Wall was forced open. On that night, a 35-year-old East German named Angela Merkel crossed into West Berlin. In November 2005, this woman became Germany's Chancellor and was re-elected again in 2009 and 2013. Having grown up in former East Germany, Merkel understood the limitations and the tyranny promulgated by communism. Under capitalism, she has witnessed a rapid transformation and significant rise in living standards in former East Germany.

Policies That Work

When I was a junior at Canisius High School in Buffalo, New York in the late 1970s, I traveled to Washington, D.C. to interview my Congressman, Jack Kemp, for a paper I was writing on the Kemp-Roth Bill, formally known as the Economic Recovery Tax Act of 1981. I remember my first encounter with the Congressman well. He enthusiastically pulled me aside, gave me several books to read, and explained how lower tax rates generate higher economic growth, and in turn, lead to more tax revenue. This conviction, advanced by economist Arthur Laffer and his famous Laffer Curve, helped shaped my view of economics and tax policy. It apparently also influenced the view of many policymakers, including Ronald Reagan. Jack Kemp passed away in 2009 at age 73.

When he took office in 1981, Reagan inherited an economy that, up until then, was in the worst recession since the Great Depression. Unemployment and inflation were both running in double digits. And the mood of the country was poor at best. As a result, Reagan had campaigned on a platform of change. Similarly, President Obama inherited an economy mired deep in recession. And, like Reagan, President Obama campaigned on the promise to implement change. But the change President Reagan and President Obama advocated was, in many ways, very different.

Both saw change as necessary, but both approached it from seemingly opposite directions. This reminds me of a quote by Winston Churchill, who said,

"There is nothing wrong with change, if it's in the right direction."

In August 1981, President Reagan signed the Kemp-Roth Bill into law. It slashed marginal earned income tax rates by 25 percent across the board over a period of three years. Plus, the marginal tax rate on unearned income was cut from 70 percent to 50 percent immediately. The tax rate on capital gains was immediately decreased from 28 percent to 20 percent. Importantly, President Reagan championed free trade. The results: from 1983 through 1986, U.S. economic growth rose to an average of nearly 5 percent annually — up from less than 1 percent in real terms from 1978 through 1982.

As previously noted, Reagan also understood the importance of lifting morale and consistently invoked our country's greatness. He inspired Americans and boosted their level of confidence. This had a beneficial effect that should not be underestimated.

Overall, President Reagan's policies had a very positive impact on the United States. But they were not perfect.

The global recession that began in the United States in 2008 revealed flaws in the American system of free market capitalism that were set in motion years prior. In turn, free market capitalism became the focus of much criticism. In July 2009, Roger Altman, Deputy Secretary of the Treasury during the first Clinton administration, said for 30 years the American model of free market capitalism spread across the globe. In turn, the role of the state had diminished, and deregulation, privatization and the openness of borders to capital and trade increased. However, since the recession began, Altman said, the American system is largely seen as having failed and concluded that economic globalization — the dynamic process that involves the integration of national markets through international trade and investment, and powered by advances in telecommunications, transportation and finance — was in retreat both in concept and in practice, and global economic and financial integration were reversing. In addition, he said the role of the state, together with financial and trade protectionism, was ascending. Unfortunately, he was right.

Over decades, this American system known as the Margaret Thatcher-Ronald Reagan model delivered a remarkably higher quality of life than competing systems for billions of people worldwide. Why? Perhaps because this brand promotes free markets and less government control as opposed to other systems characterized by greater state control and a focus on wealth redistribution. Margaret Thatcher, Prime Minister of the United

Kingdom from 1979 to 1990, and Ronald Reagan stressed the efficiency of private enterprise, liberalized trade and relatively open markets. This led to policy decisions that advanced the recent era of greater global integration. And contrary to what many believe, the results have been positive.

Unfortunately, during the Great Recession, confidence in free market capitalism fell to the depths of the Dow Jones Industrial Average. Many factors were responsible, including poor assumptions based on rising real estate values, combined with the wide availability of capital at extremely low interest rates. And what will be remembered did occur: greedy financial wizards packaged and sold dubious financial instruments that were subject to little or no government oversight. However, in remedying these defects, it is essential not to destroy the elements that have enabled America to achieve so much.

For example, noted earlier, fundamental to American economic success is Joseph Schumpeter's "creative destruction." Our free market capitalist system, which constantly produces new and more advanced products, services, technologies, and organizations, also displaces American jobs. If the advantages of "creative destruction" are not thoughtfully grasped, the introduction of elaborate regulations designed to prevent job displacements or future economic crises could have unintended consequences, like preventing the process of "creative destruction" from doing its long-term beneficial job.

TOO BIG TO SUCCEED

During and after the height of the financial crisis, we constantly heard why some of the largest and most interconnected businesses were "too big to fail." But by increasing the size of the federal government, and more importantly, the size of its spending packages and "helpful" programs, the entire process becomes too big to manage and ultimately, too big to succeed. Since government service providers have no competition, a primary factor that makes capitalism so successful, there's little oversight and accountability, and little drive or incentive to become more efficient, more productive, more innovative, and more creative.

As stated by John Steele Gordon, author of *An Empire of Wealth: The Epic History of American Economic Power*, "Politicians can only make political decisions, not economic ones. They are, after all, first and foremost in the re-election business. Because of the need to be re-elected, politicians are always likely to have a short-term bias. What looks good right now is more important to politicians than long-term consequences even when those consequences can be easily foreseen."

Our free enterprise system is responsible for creating jobs and wealth in the United States. And it has done so for generations. Surprising to many, the U.S. share of world economic output has remained somewhat consistent over the years. According the Economic Research Service of the United States Department of Agriculture, which compares economic statistics of 190 countries, in 1970 U.S. GDP output represented 25.39 percent of world output. By 2014, this had only dropped to 22.68 percent, a minor decline considering the tremendous output of China alone in the last decade.

Government control, with its tremendous size and its unintended consequences, could seriously undermine this system, as well as its wealth and job-creating capacities. Daniel Mitchell from the Cato Institute said once government expands beyond a certain level, there tends to be an inverse relationship between the size of government and economic growth. Have we reached this point? In an October 15, 2014 *Wall Street Journal* op-ed, Brian Wesbury, Chief Economist at First Trust Portfolios put it well. He said, "The larger the slice taken by the government, the smaller the size left over for the private sector, which means fewer jobs and a lower standard of living."

We must not forget that the ability of our government to provide services and care for those that can't care for themselves is limited by the private sector's ability to grow the economy and generate wealth. If the private sector falters, the resources provided by the government are directly effected.

Dating back to the Revolutionary War, Americans always have questioned the authority, wisdom and efficiency of government bureaucracy and control. Plus, the U.S. business community has always maintained a high level of independence and rejected invitations from government to cozy up. In turn, attempts to establish industrial policy in the United States, which typically requires the government to select winners and losers, are resisted. I believe this is a good thing.

Nevertheless, limited government-led efforts to improve and refine our economic system should be welcomed in order to compete with those countries where industry is supported by the state. From France to Japan to China, many countries throughout the world have established, to varying degrees, government-business working relationships that have jointly funded business expansion and the creation of new technologies.

As a result, many American companies are not just competing against foreign companies — they are competing against foreign governments. Leveling the playing field is a worthy objective. But fundamentally altering American free market capitalism, a primary factor that has made the United States the envy of the world, likely will create new economic realities that could negatively impact our quality of life and change America's business environment for decades to come.

Decisions We Must Make

During the height of the financial crisis, many Americans believed the United States would survive and even emerge stronger. And as early as October 2008, Warren Buffett, one of the world's wealthiest men and greatest investors of all time, reaffirmed that the financial world, both in the United States and abroad, was a mess. Yet, in the same *New York Times* op-ed, the Oracle of Omaha also said now was the time to buy U.S. equities. What did Buffett know that others didn't?

"In the twentieth century, the United States endured two world wars and other traumatic and expensive military conflicts; the Depression; a dozen or so recessions and financial panics; oil shocks; a flu epidemic; and the resignation of a disgraced president. Yet the Dow rose from 66 to 11,497," he said. What Mr. Buffett knew, we also know: America always gets back on its feet, regardless of how hard it's been knocked down. And we've proven it time and time again.

America is a land of entrepreneurial people who believe anything is possible if we put our collective mind to it. We also are flexible and dynamic. We know how to adapt to change and adjust to new challenges. Foreigners recognize this as well. As a result, America continues to be the destination of the world's hungry, as well as the world's brightest entrepreneurs, engineers and scientists. Interestingly, even though the 2008 global financial crisis began in the United States, foreigners still felt America was the safest destination for their hard earned capital and began transferring it here in large amounts. As a result, the value of the U.S. dollar actually strengthened as the crisis worsened.

Foreigners sometimes have more faith in the United States than Americans. Thus, only 64 percent of respondents from a December 2014 *New York Times* survey said they continued to believe in the "American dream," the lowest percentage in nearly two decades. I believe the "American dream," which took a temporary respite due to the worst recession since the Great Depression, will continue if we make the right choices in the years ahead.

The "American dream," a state of being popularized by James Truslow Adams in 1931, is one in which "life should be better and richer and fuller for everyone, with opportunity for each according to ability or achievement." Continued by Adams, "It is not a dream of motor cars and high wages merely, but a dream of social order in which each man and each woman shall be able to attain to the fullest stature of which they are innately capable, and be recognized by others for what they are, regardless of the fortuitous circumstances of birth or position."

Part of being American is accepting that failure is part of a successful process. Horatio Alger, a nineteenth century American author who wrote "rags to riches" stories, illustrated how poor kids achieved the American Dream through hard work, courage, determination and concern for others. This truly American cultural and social ideal remains embodied in the American psyche. It gives people hope and confidence that in America anything is possible. And this optimism often empowers Americans to reach further.

Fear, as witnessed during the recent financial crisis, immobilizes and seizes all creativity. And who knew this better than Franklin D. Roosevelt? In his first inaugural address on March 4, 1933, when the Great Depression had reached its depth, he said, "This great nation will endure as it has endured, will revive and will prosper. So, first of all, let me assert my firm belief that the only thing we have to fear is fear itself." Franklin Roosevelt was right then, and continues to be right. The U.S. possesses tremendous strengths. When faced with difficult challenges, America always has risen to the occasion. But successes achieved in the past do not guarantee success in the future.

Following World War II, the entire global strategy of the United States was summed up in one word: containment. The goal was clear and simple: to contain the military, political, and ideological advances of communism. This clear-cut struggle was the glue that held America and its allies together, and it was a major factor in decisions affecting international trade and relations. Since the end of the Cold War, we no longer live in a bipolar world where a balance of power exists between the United States and the Soviet Union. However, since the end of the Cold War, the world has moved to a state of disorder similar to that at the beginning of the 19th century.

Today, our leadership is asking some of the same questions we asked back then. Do we embrace American free market capitalism or move toward a more socialist model as many politicians on the left advocate? Do we embrace global integration as we have in the past or reject it and move toward a protectionist position?

Should American business establish a closer relationship with the government or resist it?

How we answer these questions will effect virtually every American, and impact long-term economic growth, opportunity, and the ability to compete with countries across the globe for generations to come.

WAYS TO STIR
THE SECRET SAUCE

When I entered Canisius High School in Buffalo, New York, our football team was on a winning streak that stretched well before I arrived. Prior to each game, our coach often spoke about our consecutive winning seasons and reminded us that our undefeated record was not guaranteed simply because we donned Canisius football jerseys. This overconfidence is not limited to sports.

Many successful companies assume that since they have beat market expectations for lengthy periods of time, it's virtually assured that they will continue to do so. But many forget why. Similarly, the United States has achieved remarkable results for generations. Many assume this will continue — not understanding the factors that have made this country truly exceptional.

In recent years the United States government has become dysfunctional, establishing deep divisions not experienced in the lifetimes of many. Our leadership's failure to lead has resulted in one manufactured crisis after another and weakened the American system. In time it will become evident whether the results of the November 2014 midterm elections — where the Republican Party took control of the Senate and strengthened its majority in the House of Representatives — have an impact on this problem.

Noted earlier, the inability of Congress and President Obama to effectively deal with the debt ceiling, government shutdown, fiscal cliff and sequester has raised serious questions and caused citizens to re-think their political positions and party loyalties. And the government's failure to reform the tax code, invest in infrastructure, restructure entitlement programs, seriously tackle immigration, or initiate a debate on how to improve education has resulted in little confidence in the government. This has created uncertainty for companies in terms of future corporate liabilities or the direction of fiscal and monetary policy. In response, corporate America has held onto cash, investing at a slower pace partly due to the level of uncertainty caused by government gridlock.

How to Educate Policymakers

Moving forward, it's imperative that elected officials pass policies designed to enhance American competitiveness, promote economic growth, and create jobs. It's also essential that policymakers support legislation that advances global economic integration by passing trade liberalizing legislation that further opens foreign markets.

In addition, stated by the McKinsey Global Institute, policymakers "will need a clear understanding of how technology might shape the global economy and society over the coming decade. They will need to decide how to invest in new forms of education and infrastructure, and figure out how disruptive economic change will affect comparative advantages. Governments will need to create an environment in which citizens can continue to prosper, even as emerging technologies disrupt their lives."

To achieve these goals, it's necessary to educate elected officials on what is at stake and on the policies that will help ensure America continues to move forward — not backward.

To do so, it's wise to establish grassroots coalitions designed to educate elected officials, as well as the general public and the media on a long-term basis. To ensure success, coalitions need to be well organized and operate on a permanent basis. And when selecting participants, coalitions should include individuals, employers and employees who share common beliefs and interests, as well as influential community members. But to achieve a truly broad-based coalition, opinion leaders, academics, students, business associations and other organizations who understand the importance of economic growth and global engagement should be invited to participate.

To get the message out in a compelling manner and win the support of policymakers, it's important for coalitions to:

- Research, write and publish position papers,
- Coordinate meetings between policymakers and coalition members to discuss the positions and the impact on local companies, employees and communities,
- Encourage coalition members to submit op-eds to local newspapers that explain the importance of your positions, and recognize the efforts of policymakers who already have supported them,
- Encourage coalition members to attend newspaper editorial board meetings to explain the positions,
- Generate letter-writing campaigns to encourage policymakers to advance the positions or to thank those who have already supported them,
- Obtain quotes from coalition members expressing the importance of the positions to their companies and workers, and in turn,

provide them to policymakers and/or include them in op-eds,

- Educate newspaper reporters on your position in an attempt to generate positive or balanced articles, and

- Sponsor educational events that promote your positions.

To ensure success, it is important to assist members of the coalition with talking points, as well as sample drafts of letters and op-eds. And in order to get all boats moving upstream together, it is vital to compromise when necessary, focusing on common interests while setting aside differences.

Why is this so important? Coalitions that advocate anti-business and anti-global engagement policies are gaining in number. And during this period of poor economic growth and elevated unemployment, these organizations are putting even greater pressure on Members of Congress. Although well-intentioned, this pressure can and has resulted in anti-growth positions that result in fewer, not more American jobs.

Interestingly, national coalitions that operate at the district level are becoming more effective and have a significant collective impact on the positions of Members of Congress. As this trend builds, the effectiveness of Washington, D.C.-based lobbyists may be declining. Why? Inside the D.C. beltway tens of thousands of lobbyists compete for the attention of policymakers. Distinguishing their messages and the degree of importance each one has on constituents back home is increasingly difficult for policymakers. As a result, D.C.-based lobbyists are finding it harder to acquire the attention of politicians.

For these and other reasons, messages initiated from districts that are championed by political supporters and friends of the policymaker, as well as local employers and employees, are becoming increasingly potent. This is no surprise since "the squeaky wheel gets the grease." And as this retail method amplifies its message, Members of Congress can't ignore the greater input from their constituents.

Since the early 1990s, I and others have managed numerous coalitions, including those established to support passage of the North American Free Trade Agreement (NAFTA), the GATT Uruguay Round Agreements, Fast Track Negotiating Authority, China Most Favored Nation trade status (MFN), China Normal Trade Relations status (NTR), China Permanent Normal Trade Relations status (PNTR), and Trade Promotion Authority (TPA). In the end, the Congressional votes needed were obtained. But it was not easy.

Our success was partly accomplished by educating thousands of members of the business community as to the benefits of international business on their companies, employees and communities. Through phone calls and letters sent to Members of Congress, meetings with policymakers and their staffs, op-eds placed in local newspapers, favorable or balanced articles written by reporters, editorial endorsements from editorial-page editors, and countless radio shows, etc., our coalitions confidently expressed their support for the legislation we were seeking.

The result: during a 10 month period, our national media campaign designed to support a particular bill in Congress resulted in 75 op-eds placed, 24 Letters to the Editor placed, 64 editorial board meetings, 56 public/media events, and 25 articles crediting our organization. In addition, during this period our coalition also achieved 384 face-to-face meetings with Members of Congress, 178 face-to-face meetings with Congressional staffers, 30 public forum questions asked, 5,245 letters and faxes sent to Members of Congress, 544 e-mails sent to Members of Congress, 230 phone calls made to Members of Congress, and 745 phone calls made to Congressional staffers.

Additionally, our national coalition distributed 69,411 reports, and worked with the business community to place 84 articles in association mailings and 25 articles in employee newsletters. Our impact was broad and our messages reached numerous policy makers at critical stages in the legislative process. The efforts of our coalition during this campaign resulted in passage of the legislation in the House of Representatives by a margin of almost 55 percent.

Of the 124 Members of Congress targeted by our coalition, 81 voted favorably. This represented 65 percent of Members targeted — a 20 percent higher approval rate over the House vote. And those were among the more difficult legislators to persuade. Of the 57 Republicans targeted, 48 favored the legislation. This represented 84 percent of Republicans targeted. Of the 67 Democrats targeted, 33 favored the legislation. This represented 49 percent. From its modest beginnings in a handful of states, our coalition expanded to include more than two dozen states, and it reached 329 House districts and 50 United States Senators. This represented 76 percent of House Members and 50 percent of Senators.

How to Communicate the Message

Several decades ago, as Albert Einstein monitored an exam for a graduate physics class, a student raised his hand and said there was a problem: the questions on the exam were the same as the previous year's test. Einstein agreed. The questions were indeed the same, but in a year's time the answers had changed completely. Given the accelerated pace of change, the "answers" are not just different from those of last year. In many cases, they are different from those of last month and last week.

Whether you are providing answers or explaining and defending a position to a Member of Congress, a state assembly member, newspaper reporter, investors, or employees, it's essential to be up-to-date on events and facts. And the ability to effectively communicate the right message is paramount. It can help to achieve greater understanding, acceptance and support or result in bad press, policymakers running for cover, low employee morale, and decreased investor confidence.

To truly achieve understanding, it is important to frame or position an issue in a context the audience can easily grasp. For example, when discussing a particular issue, it is important to explain it in terms we all value: our homes and family, career opportunities, wage potential, and quality of life. Attempting to discuss issues solely in economic, theoretical or non-emotional terms is likely to result in a lack of understanding or limited engagement on the part of the target audience.

Just as important, it is essential to keep the message simple. To do so, narrowly focus on the goal.

Unfortunately, when complex issues are discussed or responses to questions are provided to the media, policymakers, employees or investors, the communicator often attempts to convey too much information — creating confusion and new objections.

In the end, the audience may not have the background, possess the necessary level of detail or connect all the dots. And even if the target audience is fully up to speed on every aspect, they may only retain 20 percent of what is expressed. The solution is not to repeat the points five times, but rather, to prioritize your answers with the most concise and compelling information available.

Furthermore, keeping the message simple and concise also will allow you to communicate it in little time. And since you are likely to only have a few seconds to convey a compelling argument on radio or television, few alternatives exist. And remember, credibility is key. Manage expectations and do not oversell what is realistically anticipated to occur based on a corporate decision or response to globalization.

When dealing with newspapers, magazines, radio and television organizations, as well as electronic and online media, it is imperative to understand one key thing: the media is bombarded with information daily. This information comes in numerous forms, such as news releases from companies and community groups, announcements from local, state and federal government agencies, and stories from wire services, like Associated Press International.

This enormous and overwhelming amount of information cannot possibly be covered in the press. So what makes the media select some stories over others? Simply put, reporters like unique, interesting and especially controversial stories that relate to their readers' lives. Unfortunately, quite often the media may be quick to decide that any announcement regarding an organization's position could mean bad news for the public. As a result, when communicating your decisions, be sure to let reporters know exactly how they will impact employees and local communities.

Today's media works more quickly than ever before. Racing against the clock and competing with instantaneous information channels, the media does not have any time to waste. That's why it's important to respect the media's time constraints. In general, the best time of day to contact a news desk is early to mid-morning, but many reporters also work evenings. When in doubt, prior to sending any information to the media, call the reporter to introduce yourself and find out what is best for his or her schedule.

Reporters need to grasp the central idea of a story,

understand what makes it newsworthy, and put it into words and images their audience can easily understand. As a result, the best approach to take with the media is to be honest, upfront and sincere. If you consistently tell the plain and simple truth to reporters in the most prompt manner possible — even when the news may be sensitive or controversial — you will help your position beyond compare. And, if you demonstrate respect for a reporter's time, job requirements and position, chances are he or she will treat you in kind.

Very importantly, in order to effectively respond to sensitive issues that could impact your interests, it is essential to have an in-depth understanding of the subject, its leverage points, emotional hot buttons, likely objections and the talking points required to successfully overcome those objections. In determining how to address various issues, proceed with a process I describe as riding the "logic train." In discussing the dimensions of a particular topic, a flow of logic may drive the train in a particular direction. After more debate, an important point or obstacle may turn the train in another direction. And after even more deliberation, the train may turn on a totally different track. The benefits of this analysis are tremendous.

In addition to considering a variety of perspectives, the experience of riding the logic train reveals a multitude of issues not initially considered relevant. In the end, by looking at a topic from 360 degrees, you will be prepared to confidently and persuasively discuss the most controversial issues. This may be tantamount to playing chess—with a focus on the next four moves.

In addition to the groups noted, it's also important to keep employees and investors informed and in the loop. Perhaps the most important thing to remember is that employees and investors should always be informed of decisions and announcements prior to the news media whenever possible. Nothing destroys a company's credibility more quickly than when employees or investors, or even customers, learn about company news from an outside source.

Although many of the same concepts utilized when working with the media apply when communicating with employees and investors, such as being honest and sincere, creating strong relationships, demonstrating mutual respect, understanding the other's point of view and time constraints, and not being afraid to admit you do not know something, there are some differences that exist.

One difference is the way in which you communicate the message and the vehicle you use to share information. While the media primarily depends on interviews, employees and investors usually expect written forms of communication, and on a more frequent basis. For employees, this means you can use your company's internal publication/employee newsletter, intranet or internal email system, employee paychecks or even special home mailings to communicate information and company policies. In the case of investors, who may often be the last to believe that change is necessary, quarterly earnings statements, annual reports and specialized mailings may be used.

Additional ways to communicate with your employees and investors include specially designed videos, town meetings with a question and answer format, and open forums. But no matter which way you choose to communicate, the most important things to do are keep employees and investors informed, be fully honest to combat the creation of rumors, do not make promises you cannot keep and do your best to outline the positives that will result from your organization's decisions. Your audiences may be skeptical or hostile, so it is imperative you remain poised and create an atmosphere of cooperation with a sincere intent to be helpful.

In general, employees and investors are crucial audiences and you must communicate with them just as vigorously as you do with the media, if not more so. Employees and investors who respect management, take pride in the company's products or services, and believe they are being treated with dignity and respect are imperative to a company's success.

ENDNOTES

CHAPTER ONE: THE PERILS OF GROWING UP IN A HIGH-TECH WORLD

1. James Manyika, et.al., "Disruptive Technologies: Advances that Will Transform Life, Business and the Global Economy," McKinsey Global Institute, May 2013, p43.

2. Ibid, p6.

3. Cushman & Wakefield, "Facing the Millennial Wave," 2012, p2.

4. Deloitte, "Manufacturing Opportunity: A Deloitte Series on Making America Stronger," 2012.

5. U.S. Bureau of Labor Statistics., "Women in the Labor Force: A Databook," May 2014, p1.

6. Neil Shah, "More Young Stay Put in the Biggest Cities," *The Wall Street Journal*, January 20, 2015.

7. McKinsey & Company, "The Economic Impact of Achievement of the Achievement Gap in America's Schools," April 2009, p17.

CHAPTER TWO: JOBS, EDUCATION AND THE RIGHT STUFF

1. James Manyika, et al., "An Economy that Works: Job Creation and America's Future," McKinsey Global Institute, June 2011, p1.

2. National Center for Education Statistics, U.S. Department of Education, Table 104.20.

3. College Board, "Trends in College Pricing," 2014, p16.

4. College Parents of America and National Student Clearinghouse.

5. Vivek Wadhwa, et al., "Education, Entrepreneurship and Immigration: America's New Immigrant Entrepreneurs, Part II," Duke University, June 2017, p2.

6. U.S. Department of Homeland Security, U.S. Immigration and Customs Enforcement, "Sevis by the Numbers," February 2015.

7. Ibid.

8. Peter Downs, "Can't Find Skilled Workers? Start an Apprentice Program," *The Wall Street Journal*, January 16, 2014.

9. National Center for Education Statistics, U.S. Department of Education, Table 502.30.

10. New York Federal Reserve, "Current Issues in Economics," November 3, 2014.

CHAPTER THREE: THE DIRECTION OF ECONOMIC GROWTH

1. CoreLogic, "CoreLogic Equity Report," First Quarter 2015.

2. Anders Aslund, "Why Growth in Emerging Markets Is Likely to Fall," Peterson Institute for International Economics, November 2013, p4.

CHAPTER FOUR: U.S. PRODUCTION AND ABUNDANT ENERGY

1. Theodore H. Moran and Lindsay Oldenski, "The U.S. Manufacturing Base: Signs of Strength," Peterson Institute for International Economics, June 2014, p2.

2. James Manyika, et al., "Manufacturing the Future: The Next Era of Global Growth and Innovation," November 2012, McKinsey Global Institute, p7.

3. Theodore H. Moran and Lindsay Oldenski," "The U.S. Manufacturing Base: Signs of Strength," Peterson Institute for International Economics, June 2014, p2.

4. Ibid, p8.

5. Adam Posen, "The Errors of Conservatives Obscure the Case for Trade," *Financial Times*, January 22, 2014.

6. U.S. Energy Information Administration, http://www.eia.gov.

7. U.S. Energy Information Administration, "Annual Energy Outlook 2014," Early Release Overview, p12.

8. U.S. Energy Information Administration, http://www.eia.gov

9. John F. Kennedy School of Government, Harvard University, "Oil: The Next Revolution," June 2012, p13.

10. U.S. Energy Information Administration, http://www.eia.gov.

11. Ibid.

12. Ibid.

13. IHS, "America's New Energy Future: The Unconventional Oil and Gas Revolution and the U.S. Economy," September 2013, p15.

14. John F. Kennedy School of Government, Harvard University, "Oil: The Next Revolution," June 2012, p14.

15. IHS, "America's New Energy Future: The Unconventional Oil and Gas Revolution and the U.S. Economy," September 2013, p41.

16. Ibid, p15.

17. Ibid.

18. Harold L. Sirkin, Michael Zinser and Justin Rose, "Behind the American Export Surge," Boston Consulting, August 2013, p3.

19. Ibid.

CHAPTER FIVE:
GLOBALIZATION IS LIKE FIRE

1. Matthew J. Slaughter, "The Free-Trade Way to Job Growth," *The Wall Street Journal*, October, 2 2014.

2. Office of the United States Trade Representative, "The President's 2015 Trade Agenda," 2015.

3. Margareta Drzeniek Hanouz, Thierry Geiger, and Sean Doherty, eds., "The Global Enabling Trade Report 2014," World Economic Forum, Geneva, 2014

4. Simon J. Evenett, "Beggar They Neighbor," Global Trade Alert, Centre for Economic Policy Research, London, UK, 2014, p10.

CHAPTER SEVEN: THE FUTURE OF A
U.S.-CHINA DOMINATED WORLD

1. Kenneth L. Kraemer, Greg Linden, and Jason Dedrick, "Capturing Value in Global Networks: Apple's iPad and iPhone," University of California, Irvine, University of California, Berkeley and Syracuse University, July 2011.

INDEX